Marilyn
ON LOCATION

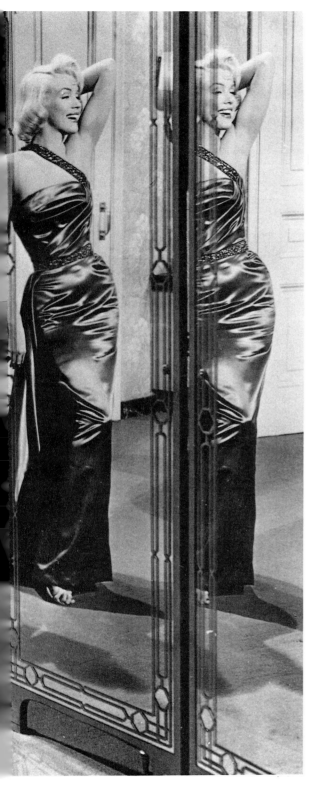

Marilyn
ON LOCATION

BART MILLS

SIDGWICK & JACKSON
LONDON

Also by Bart Mills:
MICKEY ROURKE

First published in Great Britain in 1989
by Sidgwick & Jackson Limited

Copyright © 1989 by Bart Mills

ISBN 0-283-99766-4

Designed by Roger Walker

Typeset by Rowland Phototypesetting Limited,
Bury St Edmunds, Suffolk

Printed by
Butler and Tanner Limited, Frome, Somerset

for Sidgwick & Jackson Limited
1 Tavistock Chambers, Bloomsbury Way,
London WC1A 2SG

FRONTISPIECE: *HOW TO MARRY A MILLIONAIRE.* (NATIONAL FILM ARCHIVE, LONDON)

Contents

ONE

'The best you can get from me'

THE QUINTESSENTIAL MARILYN OF THE EARLY 1950S IN *GENTLEMEN PREFER BLONDES*. (NATIONAL FILM ARCHIVE, LONDON)

*W*rap parties were always the most awkward. At the end of shooting any Marilyn Monroe film, the cast and crew weren't in any mood to forgive and forget. Hours, days, sometimes weeks of waiting around for Marilyn to arrive, to get ready to act and then to remember her lines would have pushed even those who started out feeling sympathetic towards her into a mood of black resentment, leading to a desire never to work on one of her films again.

Today, twenty-seven years after her death, most of those who worked with Marilyn say that the final product was always worth it. After all, few in the audience for Marilyn's films cared how difficult the films were to make. When her performance reached the screen, her co-workers generally said they'd forgotten the difficulties they'd had dealing with her. Exasperation and irritation softened into acceptance and even admiration. After her death it was even harder to remember how roundly she was disliked by those close to her.

But immediately after a Monroe film wrapped, when those employed to make it customarily gathered at a party to cement or break off relationships formed during the three months or so they'd been working together, everyone unloaded on Marilyn. Condemnations from groups promoting decency and motherhood were mild compared with the opinions of those who had suffered daily contact with her.

So Marilyn would not appear. For one thing, she typically arrived at any party when most guests were leaving. Aside from her chronic procrastination, Marilyn avoided parties because they were just additional occasions for ogling, and if there were no direct professional benefits for her, there was no reason to go. Sometimes she was pointedly not invited, as after Billy Wilder's *Some Like It Hot* wrapped. Another time she put in a stage-managed appearance to apologize for her behaviour during filming, at the end of Laurence Olivier's *The Prince and the Showgirl*.

However, there was no wrap party after shooting stopped on her last film, *Something's Got to Give*. 20th Century-Fox fired Marilyn after obtaining just one week's worth of usable footage in three weeks of filming, and then cancelled the film altogether. Instead of a wrap party with wallets bulging, the 'little people' on the film were out of work. They expressed their feelings in an advertisement they bought in the Hollywood trade papers ironically 'thanking' Marilyn. Eight weeks later, on 5 August 1962, Marilyn died after taking an overdose of sleeping pills.

☐　　☐　　☐

Today, the 1950s live on in retro-chic. If the 1960s was the decade of up-heaval and the 1970s was the decade that didn't happen, the 1980s is surely the decade when we wish we were again living in the 1950s. At Hollywood memorabilia sales, artefacts of Marilyn's life sell best. Andy Warhol's silk-screened multiple portrait of her recently changed hands at $4 million.

THE EARLY STARLET IN A SCENE FROM THE 1951 FILM, *AS YOUNG AS YOU FEEL.* (NATIONAL FILM ARCHIVE, LONDON)

MARILYN IN *BUS STOP* – HER FIRST FILM AFTER BEGINNING CLASSES AT THE ACTORS STUDIO IN NEW YORK. (KOBAL COLLECTION)

The 1950s was the first decade that came in colour. Jean Harlow had been blonde, but fans of her black-and-white movies had to take it mainly on trust. When Marilyn hired Harlow's old peroxidist to bleach her roots every Saturday, the result glowed yellow-white on screen. Marilyn was so aware of her hair colour and her status as the blondest of the blondes that several times, as on the sets of *Bus Stop* and *Something's Got to Give*, she attempted to have the hair of supporting actresses darkened.

The 1950s was a blatant decade: cars grew fins; neon signs became an art form; pop music discovered the electric guitar and turned into rock and roll; the Yankees won the pennant year after year after year; and the Russians exploded record mega-tonnage of nuclear weapons. In the 1950s, if it could be done, it was overdone. Nudity became conceivable in mass circulation magazines. Sex scenes in films progressed beyond chaste, clothed embraces. Spectacle and overstatement became the norm in films as the industry sought to provide what its new competitor, TV, couldn't.

Not until publicists captured the White House in the 1980s had publicity held so strong a relation to content as it did in the 1950s. After the privations and dangers of the 1940s, when reality on the front page every day was unavoidable, people craved illusions. American power and prosperity will never wane because America is always in the right: we like Ike; everybody everywhere wants to drink Coke; Negroes actually prefer segregation; LS/MFT – Lucky Strike means fine tobacco; women in a man's world can only be mistresses or housewives; cars need more and more horsepower; better living through chemistry; Elvis enjoys being in the army; movies are better than ever; Alan Ladd is tall; and Rock Hudson is straight.

At the height of America's susceptibility to publicity, when there were fewer movies and hence fewer movie stars than in earlier decades, before the press was interested in TV stars, 20th Century-Fox promoted Marilyn and Marilyn promoted Marilyn. In her starlet days, she was tireless in her cultivation of the press. Her most reliable escort was a journalist, Sidney Skolsky. She was always available to pose, whether at sessions or for candids, and she always had a new and more revealing outfit to pose in. In 1951 and 1952, before she had starred in even one film, she was already famous for her sexy stills and her cute remarks. Her name became a catch-phrase meaning 'bimbo'. At Hollywood awards ceremonies and other gatherings, she would stage-manage a late and spectacular entrance and monopolize the next day's press coverage. Once when she appeared at an awards dinner in a skin-tight dress from which 'her tits popped out like two watermelons' (as Clark Gable testified), Joan Crawford sounded off to the press about Marilyn's 'shocking display of bad taste'. Maybe so, but it was Marilyn's picture in the papers, not Crawford's.

By the middle of the decade, she was the most recognizable star in Hollywood. The frenzied peak was reached in 1954–55, when her split from Joe DiMaggio was front-page news at the same time as Fox was assiduously marketing the still from *The Seven Year Itch* showing her standing over a subway grating, her skirt billowing around her waist, her face suffused with pleasure at her own exhibitionism. The still was far more provocative than the scene in the film it purported to illustrate. The film itself turned out to be a delight and a success, but that didn't alter the fact that Marilyn was always more famous for being Marilyn than for the roles she played in her films. The extent to which her image eventually eclipsed the reality was recognized by Arthur Miller, who wrote of her last years, 'She was "Marilyn Monroe", and that was what was killing her.'

America's mood altered subtly in Eisenhower's second term, and the public's perception of Marilyn changed too. In 1957 Sputnik showed America lagging Russia in space; the economy stumbled in the recession of 1958; a few black people in the South started demanding their rights; an American U-2 spy plane was shot down over Russia; Castro's revolution in Cuba damaged American prestige; the beats disturbed the smug American literary scene; and new artistic ideas began seeping in from Europe.

Marilyn's desertion of Hollywood during 1955 and her interest in broadening her range coincided with these other more sober trends. Much of the public reaction to her new career goals was epitomized by the reporter at a press conference who ridiculed her expressed desire to appear in a film of Dostoyevsky's *The Brothers Karamazov* by asking her if she could spell the name of the character she wanted to play. Others, however, sympathized with Marilyn's effort to improve herself and advance beyond being public sex symbol number one. The message conveyed in her stills began to change slightly. Earlier, her photos held just the wanton promise of a good time; now you could also see a hint that there was a price to pay, and that she would pay it.

She was the most-photographed and most lusted-after woman in history. In the early 1950s she was simply the biggest of all the many busty Hollywood blondes of the era. Later, as America's underlying nervousness rose closer to the surface, the aspect of Marilyn that began to grip people was the angst in her sexiness. It was one thing to have a vision of a nymphomaniac, it was another to feel her sadness.

For just when she had scrambled onto the highest pedestal, she was losing her balance. She was losing it in full view of the world. Marilyn Monroe was a mentally troubled drug addict who relied on bad advice and was hounded to death by an insensitive age. Today, celebrities trumpet their rehabilitation in addiction treatment centres. Conditions like Marilyn's are now recognized as non-volitional. Addiction to prescription medicines is seen as a disease, not a wilful choice. As for Marilyn's mental troubles, they didn't fit neatly into a traditional diagnosis. She suffered from delusions, she was paranoid, she was unable to form lasting attachments, and she fixated on certain childhood feelings she never outgrew. In her later years, she was constantly under psychiatrists' care, but the treatment, which included

BUS STOP. (NATIONAL FILM ARCHIVE, LONDON)

psychoanalysis, appears to have been ineffective. Nowadays, mood-balancing drugs, like lithium carbonate, and behaviour-altering therapies might deal more successfully with ailments like Marilyn's.

Did Hollywood kill her? Stars working in movies today don't encounter the lethal combination of over-indulgence in some areas and draconian insistence on toeing the line in others. There is no star working today who could even begin to get away with Marilyn's chronic lateness and absences, nor would any modern director tolerate her inability to remember lines. The bad work habits that Marilyn developed early and in later years perfected into instruments of mass torture would in today's more professional climate be nipped in the bud. John Belushi is Marilyn's closest latter-day equivalent, but he checked his fatal excesses at the studio gate when he was working.

Today's stars, less beholden to their images, are respected as professionals in the way beautiful female stars in Marilyn's day weren't. Today's most glamorous actresses – Jessica Lange, Kim Basinger, Farrah Fawcett, among many – are freer to exercise their talent. They're not bound to studios by one-sided contracts, as Marilyn was. They're paid enough not to have money worries, as she did. They have more say in the writing and editing of their films. They work with faster film, more flexible lenses, more portable cameras and quicker make-up techniques.

Most important – and this is what makes our age so different from Marilyn's – today's stars don't have to be perfect. Standards of beauty have changed to favour the natural look. In today's films, the stars are made up to look like they're not made up. A large part of Marilyn's self-destructive procrastination involved worries about her appearance. Even when she was not rendered unfit for work by chemicals in her system, she would stare into her dressing-room mirror for hours or she would shampoo and re-set her hair over and over again, afraid to go out on the studio floor and look anything less than perfect.

Marilyn lived a heedless life. She could spend hours ignoring knocks on her dressing-room door. She never gave much thought to anything beyond her own immediate needs. Many people commented on her quick wit and native intelligence, but no one ever accused her of having any common sense. Driven by compulsions she was only dimly aware of, she was often her own worst enemy. Today we feel short-changed. Even in the few years she had, she ought to have made more films and more good films. But Hollywood was a different place three decades ago. The industry was set up to create deities and destroy them. Nowadays the fairy dust of stardom is spread over more performers, and stars needn't make their lives into a pretence. Marilyn did her best, though she disappointed many. She had one artistic credo and in everything she did, she followed it: 'Even if all I had to do in a scene was just to come in and say "Hi", I've always felt that the people ought to get their money's worth, and that this is an object of mine, to give them the best you can get from me.'

TWO

'Chewing on stray blondes'

MARILYN AS A CANNERY WORKER IN THE 1952 *CLASH BY NIGHT*. (KOBAL COLLECTION)

*I*n one of the stray snaps that survive from Marilyn's pre-Hollywood life in the northern suburbs of Los Angeles, she is standing on a beach with some other girls. She is the busty one with her eyes closed. Her smile is infectious and she seems bursting with life. She is on the chubby side, with fat cheeks and roly-poly thighs. As usual in such 'before' photos, there's nothing to indicate that this girl won't grow up to be a slatternly mother of four in a trailer camp somewhere. For a start, the baby fat will have to go, and so will the name, Norma Jean.

Norma Jean was a dreamy child. She always wanted to play make-believe games. When she listened to *The Lone Ranger* on the radio, she absorbed herself in imagining the feelings of the characters, never mind the bang-bang and clip-clop. Her mother gave her a picture of Clark Gable, and she often thought what life would be like if Gable had been her father.

As it was, she couldn't be sure who her father was. She never really settled on a last name. Norma Jean's mother was a vague and ultimately incapable woman who was in and out of mental homes during Norma Jean's childhood and eventually in again for life. The little girl was farmed out to various friends, relations and foster homes. She even spent some time in an orphanage. Instead of a mother, she was raised by a succession of 'aunts' who were not related to her.

Later, those who groped to explain Marilyn's problems looked to her unhappy childhood. Ben Hecht, the ghostwriter of a 1954 series of articles published under her byline, emphasized her orphanhood, even though her mother was in fact alive. Acutely aware of the blank in her life where a father should have been, she became fixated on the fantasy that Clark Gable was the missing man. In describing her childhood, she spoke of having narrowly escaped being raped by two men who held her down at a party. She said that when she was eight and living in one of her foster homes, a man abused her in an unspecified way that involved sitting on his lap. She told of once climbing into an open grave and examining the sky from the perspective of a corpse. She must have been a strange, troubled – and troubling – girl. After shuttling between addresses all her young life, she found herself being disposed of in a new way. Her 'Aunt' Grace arranged to marry her off to Jim Doughterty, the son of a neighbour, in June 1942. Norma Jean protested, 'But I'm too young,' but Grace answered, 'Only in years, only in years.' She was sixteen.

The first of many substitute fathers who slept in her bed, Jim Dough-erty was a good husband and provider. He worked at the Radio Plane plant in Burbank, where he had a nodding acquaintance with a hulking young co-worker named Robert Mitchum. Mitchum, who later starred with Marilyn in *River of No Return*, has often told stories about seeing a revealing photo of Norma Jean in Dougherty's wallet and about double-dating with the Doughertys. These are probably embellishments; most people claimed to know Marilyn better than they really did.

Golden Dreams

THE FAMOUS CALENDAR PICTURE. (POPPERFOTO)

When Dougherty shipped out to Shanghai with the Merchant Marines in 1944, Norma Jean went to work at the same aircraft plant as a parachute inspector. There she caught the eye of an army photographer looking for models for morale-building pictures of women filling defence plant jobs. In Monroe's lively imagination, it would be just a short step from a 'Rosie the Riveter' pose to starring in the movies. She said later, 'There was this secret in me – acting. It was like being in jail and looking at a door that said This Way Out.'

Discovering that she could make better money without her coveralls, she quit and became a model. She worked for photographers and as a 'hostess' at industrial exhibitions. At the agency's insistence, she became a blonde, and at this time she had her nose trimmed. Some of her poses from this period appeared on the covers of respectable magazines like *Family Circle*, others wound up in calendars on grease-spattered garage walls. One nude session for which she was paid $50 would help build her legend when the existence of the photos was disclosed later, in March 1952. One of the poses wound up as *Playboy*'s first centrefold in December 1953.

In Hollywood, all models aspire to be actresses. Acting ability is often beside the point in an entertainment industry so keyed to appearances. Norma Jean shed her husband, who had been absent during much of their marriage, and joined the brigade of blondes seeking a break in pictures. In Hollywood at that time, as Raymond Chandler wrote in *The Big Sleep*, 'You have to hold your teeth clamped to keep from chewing on stray blondes.' Marilyn recalled thinking that there 'must be thousands of girls sitting alone like me, dreaming of becoming a movie star. But I'm not going to worry about them. I'm dreaming the hardest.'

Howard Hughes was a devoted reader of *Laff* magazine, which often ran Norma Jean's picture. A call from him led indirectly to her getting a screen test at Fox, which signed her to a six-month contract at $75 a week, name-change included, in early 1947. Part of the deal was singing and dancing lessons, and pantomime parties with the other starlets on Saturday mornings. This was her big break and she worked hard, sometimes fore-going meals to pay for acting classes. She recalled later, 'I knew how third-rate I was. I could actually feel my lack of talent, as if it were cheap clothes I was wearing inside.'

What Norma Jean had in abundance, however, was an instinct for self-promotion. She learned to cultivate the press, realizing that her best chance to break out of the pack was to have an identity over and above being the third blonde on the left. Even before she made any movies the press was mentioning her as a comer. And she made herself available to studio executives and other powerful men.

'In Hollywood,' Marilyn wrote later, 'a girl's virtue is much less important than her hairdo. Hollywood's a place where they'll pay you $1000 for a kiss and 50 cents for your soul. I know, because I turned down the first

ORSON WELLES. (NATIONAL FILM ARCHIVE, LONDON)

offer often enough and held out for the 50 cents.' Marilyn was always ambiguous about how much she used her body to get ahead. On another occasion she said, 'You can't sleep your way into being a star, though. It takes much, much more. But it helps.'

John Huston, who was later to give Marilyn her first worthwhile film part in *The Asphalt Jungle*, recalled meeting her first on the set of his 1949 film *We Were Strangers*. Her demeanour somehow suggested to him that she was there hoping to be taken advantage of. Producer Sam Spiegel loomed. 'Something about Monroe elicited my protectiveness,' Huston remembered, so 'to forestall any hanky-panky', he promised her a screen test with John Garfield. Huston never had to deliver on the promise but prided himself on having 'saved' her from the casting couch.

Orson Welles, still a factor in Hollywood in 1947, bragged that he had an affair with Marilyn at that time. His story, given credence by his biographer Barbara Leaming, was that he was in bed with Marilyn in an upstairs room while a party was raging downstairs. A man looking for his faithless wife burst into the darkened bedroom and attacked Welles. Welles had nothing to show for it but a bruise, and he never did cast Marilyn.

There seems little doubt that Marilyn was willing to do anything to make it. Huston's gallantry, far from saving her, may even have thwarted her on that occasion. At a time when women advanced only on the whim of powerful men, Marilyn did what she had to do.

THREE

'*What did you put that fat pig in the picture for?*'

WITH CHARLES LAUGHTON IN *O. HENRY'S FULL HOUSE*. (NATIONAL FILM ARCHIVE, LONDON)

At Fox, Marilyn prepared herself for a career of playing vacuous bombshells. After months of nothing but classes and publicity work, she made her first film, *Scudda Hoo! Scudda Hay!* (Natalie Wood also appeared in a small role). When the film was released in April 1948, Marilyn was visible in just one scene. The film's principals are swimming in a lake and Marilyn is one of two girls paddling a canoe so far in the distance that only a close examination of the negative of the film has confirmed that it is her. Apparently Marilyn shot other scenes that weren't used, for there are stills of her in a farm girl costume.

In her other Fox film under that initial contract, *Dangerous Years*, Marilyn spoke her first lines. In this early warning against that 1950s bugaboo 'juvenile delinquency', Marilyn played a waitress in a soda fountain where the bad boys drop in once.

Fox had renewed Marilyn's contract once, but she failed to stand out and after a year the studio let her go. It's up or out for studio nobodies. But Marilyn had a protector, a big-time agent named Johnny Hyde, who also handled Mickey Rooney, among others. Although everyone figured the fiftyish Hyde was Marilyn's boyfriend, he may have functioned more as a father figure. He put Marilyn in a crowd scene in Rooney's 1949 *The Big Wheel*. He also got her a six-month $75-a-week contract at Columbia, where she was given a featured role in *Ladies of the Chorus*, released in 1948. She played a young chorine whose mother, also a dancer, falls for a younger man. Marilyn sang 'Every Baby Needs a Da Da Daddy' (while holding a baby doll) and 'Anyone Can Tell I Love You'. Although her singing earned Marilyn her first mention in a review ('One of the bright spots . . .' – *Motion Picture Herald*), studio boss Harry Cohn reputedly yelled to the picture's producer, 'What did you put that fat pig in the picture for? What are you doing, fucking her?' After using her just once, Columbia let her contract lapse.

It was during her one-picture stay at Columbia that Marilyn met drama coach Natasha Lytess, who remained the actress's mentor until 1955. Lytess helped Marilyn envision a career for herself that would go beyond bimbo roles. But by encouraging Marilyn to aim higher, Lytess may have triggered the pathological self-absorption that made Marilyn so hard to work with. Everyone blamed Lytess for Marilyn's excesses. Lytess was one of the most hated people in Hollywood until Marilyn left her for other mentors who became even more hated.

Hyde manoeuvred Marilyn into a tiny but attention-getting part in a 1950 Marx Brothers' vehicle, *Love Happy*. When Marilyn wobbles onscreen near the end of the movie, seeking help because 'men keep following me', smoke squirts out of Groucho's ears. The role was important despite its brevity because it showed that Marilyn wasn't just sexy; she was so sexy she was funny. This was the first time the famous Marilyn cakewalk was noticed. Her bottom jiggled like two puppies under a blanket, in James Bacon's famous phrase, as she swung her legs in little semicircles to leave a dead-

MARILYN WITH FELLOW STARLET COLLEEN TOWNSEND IN *SCUDDA HOO! SCUDDA HAY!* THIS WOULD HAVE BEEN HER FIRST SCREEN APPEARANCE HAD IT NOT BEEN CUT. (KOBAL COLLECTION)

DANGEROUS YEARS. MARILYN'S FIRST ROLE. (KOBAL COLLECTION)

LADIES OF THE CHORUS. (KOBAL COLLECTION)

WITH GROUCHO MARX IN *LOVE HAPPY*. (NATIONAL FILM ARCHIVE, LONDON)

straight track of close-together footsteps. Some, like Betty Grable, claimed to have taught Marilyn this walk by showing her how to shorten one of her high heels; others say she could do it barefoot. In any case, Groucho's reaction to it underlined Marilyn's potential to step ahead of prettier, more accomplished actresses, and attract the kind of promotion that could make her a star.

Meanwhile, though, Marilyn continued her apprenticeship in *A Ticket to Tomahawk*, *Right Cross*, *The Fireball*, *All About Eve* and *The Asphalt Jungle*, all released in 1950. *Tomahawk*, a comedy Western in which she played a chorine, gave her one duet with star Dan Dailey, 'Oh, What a Forward Young Man You Are'. *Right Cross* was a boxing picture in which Marilyn is seen on Dick Powell's arm, though he really loves June Allyson. In *The Fireball*, Marilyn was a sort of groupie who pursues roller-skating champ Mickey Rooney.

In the classic *All About Eve*, Marilyn had scenes with Bette Davis and George Sanders. She played an aspiring actress who is drama critic Sanders's 'protégée' (mistresses didn't appear in American movies for another decade). Sanders, who killed himself out of boredom in 1972, wasn't too jaded in 1950 to be dazzled by Marilyn: 'In her presence it was hard to concentrate,' he gushed. Bemused, he had the impression that 'her conversation had unexpected depths'. One thing he knew: 'What made me sure that Marilyn would eventually make it was that she so obviously needed to be a star.'

When Johnny Hyde took Marilyn into John Huston's office to try out for the role of a villainous fatcat's 'niece' in MGM's *The Asphalt Jungle*, she needed the part so much she insisted on reading her audition scene while lying on the floor. The character was supposed to recline on a divan. Marilyn was being coached by Lytess to seek out the reality of a scene, and there was no divan in Huston's office. So it appeared logical to her to lie down on the floor. Huston recollected that Marilyn got the part 'because she was damned good', although a less imaginative director might have thrown the odd young lady out.

The scene Marilyn read on the floor that day was her first in the movie. She lolls on the divan in a slinky striped pantsuit and says hardly a word. Her 'uncle' (Louis Calhern) says it all: 'Some sweet kid. Some sweet kid.' Marilyn reappears at the end of the movie when the cops come to arrest Calhern just before his getaway. 'What about my trip?' she asks, realizing there will be no getaway now. 'Don't worry, babe,' Calhern assures her. 'You'll have plenty of trips.'

'Personally, I think the best performance I ever gave was in *The Asphalt Jungle*,' Marilyn said – a comment not to be taken too seriously because at the time she said it, she was working with Huston again. Still, she was effective, and the film was a hit. 'Makes the most of her footage,' read one review of Marilyn's brief appearance. 'Plenty of trips' were indeed in the offing for her.

WITH DAN DAILEY IN *TICKET TO TOMAHAWK*. (NATIONAL FILM ARCHIVE, LONDON)

WITH DICK POWELL IN *RIGHT CROSS*. (KOBAL COLLECTION)

ANNE BAXTER, BETTE DAVIS, MARILYN MONROE, AND GEORGE SANDERS IN *ALL ABOUT EVE*. (NATIONAL FILM ARCHIVE, LONDON)

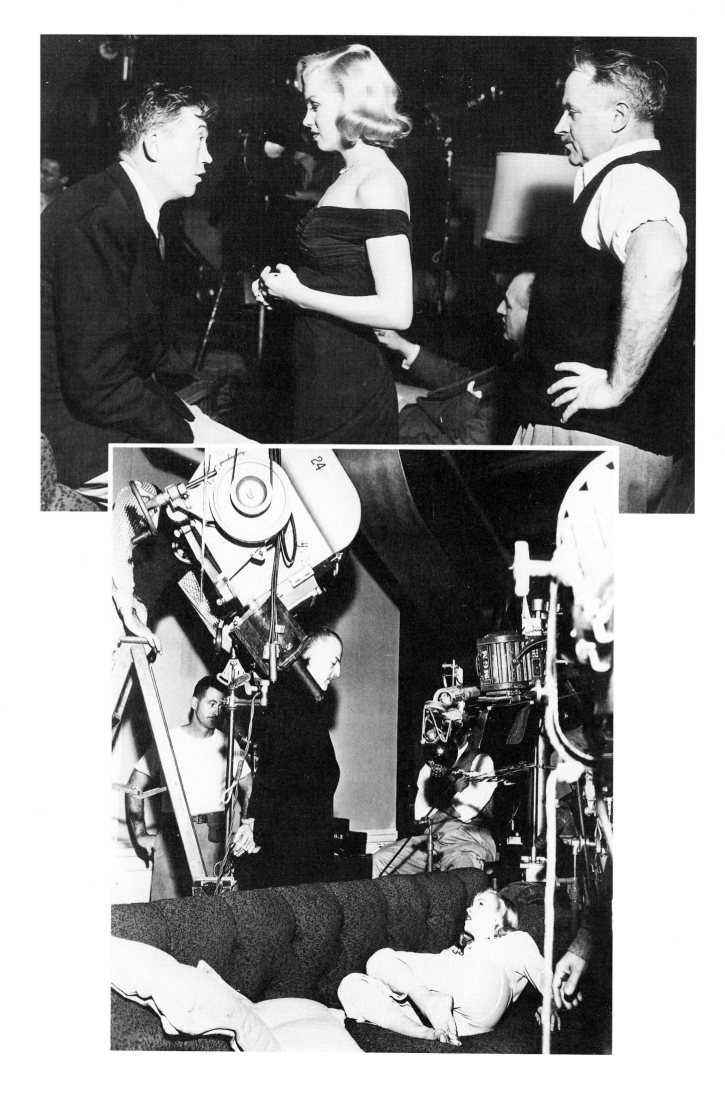

THE ASPHALT JUNGLE. WITH LOUIS CALHERN. (NATIONAL FILM ARCHIVE, LONDON)

LEFT: WITH LOUIS CALHERN. (NATIONAL FILM ARCHIVE, LONDON)

Boosted all around town by Johnny Hyde, Marilyn now rated a long-term contract at Fox. The seven-year deal she signed after making *All About Eve* for Fox was in a way a lifetime sentence for her, for she was still working off its requirements when she died.

MGM's *Hometown Story*, released in 1951, gave her extended screen time as a perky newspaper office employee. In *As Young as You Feel*, also released in 1951, she was again a secretary, rated 'superb' by *The New York Times* reviewer Bosley Crowther. This film was notable because it was on this set in 1950 that she met Arthur Miller. Her future husband visited the set with Elia Kazan, who was a friend of the film's director, Harmon Jones. Miller tells of searching through the off-camera debris before finding Marilyn sobbing in a storeroom, distraught over the death of Johnny Hyde a few days before. She had overdosed on sleeping pills on hearing the news and was still shaky. Miller was immediately smitten and hovered in her orbit for a few days. But he went back to New York and his wife, resisting temptation for five more years.

In another 1951 comedy, *Love Nest*, Marilyn was her landlord's platonic friend who innocently aroused jealousy in his wife. The film was Marilyn's first screenplay by I. A. L. Diamond. Diamond later co-wrote *Some Like It Hot*. A dyspeptic portrait of Marilyn from this period comes from another actor in *Love Nest*, Jack Paar. Paar, who later became a television talk show host and one of America's biggest stars, was nobody in 1951. Most of Paar's scenes in *Love Nest* were with Marilyn, and he bore the brunt of her unprofessional work habits. From his viewpoint low on the Fox totem pole, 'Her status at the studio with executives had little to do with her ability as an actress. She was always late and never knew her lines, yet everyone was very careful in their relation with her.'

Paar recollected one particular outrage when they were both summoned to take some publicity stills after filming ended. Marilyn was hours late – 'her usual "act",' he sneered – and when she arrived she went directly to a phone and talked for twenty minutes. Paar blew up and demanded, 'Tell that broad to get her peroxide butt over here as I am leaving in half an hour.' Paar's conclusion: 'I was quite surprised that this sad, shy, arrogant loner became a star. . . . On the set she was just another Hollywood starlet, not as attractive as many and not as likeable as most. Monroe was like a caricature of a woman. . . . I fear that beneath the façade of Monroe, there was only a frightened waitress in a diner.'

Shelley Winters, in her memoirs, *Shelley: Also Known as Shirley*, remembered Marilyn from these years more sympathetically. In Winters' recollection, she was eating in Schwab's one day, having just sent for her parents, when Marilyn joined her. 'Marilyn was carefully pouring water on a curled up straw and making it into a paper snake . . . "Gee, I wish I had somebody to send for."'

Winters also recalled a '. . . shy, very pretty blonde girl [who] used to sit

MARILYN AS SECRETARY . . . IN *HOMETOWN STORY*. (KOBAL COLLECTION)

. . . IN *AS YOUNG AS YOU FEEL*. (NATIONAL FILM ARCHIVE, LONDON)

in the corner and watch us working actresses at lunch. Her name was Norma Jean something. She rarely spoke to us, and when she did, she would whisper. She always wore halter dresses one size too small and carried around a big library book like a dictionary or encyclopaedia. . . .' Winters claimed once to have roomed with Marilyn: 'When you went to the john, she'd think you'd disappeared and she'd been left alone. She'd open up the door to see if you were still there. She was a little child.'

Still, Marilyn obviously had a future, and Fox kept casting her in sexy ingenue parts. Her next film, the 1951 *Let's Make It Legal* (co-written again by Diamond), was another 'other woman' part. It used to be commonplace for movies to follow the old stage convention of including a strong romantic subplot. Here again, in this comedy about divorce, Marilyn's character has a token relationship with the male lead (Macdonald Carey on the outs with his wife, Claudette Colbert), but actually spends more time with somebody else (moneybags Zachary Scott).

Clash by Night followed in 1952, and it used the same conventional structure, even though it was a drama (based on a Clifford Odets play), not a comedy. Marilyn's character works in a fish cannery and loves Keith Andes, who plays the brother of Barbara Stanwyck. Stanwyck eventually leaves Paul Douglas for Robert Ryan.

By this point in Marilyn's career, it had become clear to those who had to work with her that she would never become a polished professional. The presence of Lytess on the set every day was a continual annoyance to her directors, who wished Marilyn wouldn't end every take by looking towards her coach, instead of the director, for approval. Other actors resigned themselves, with varying degrees of success, to the fact that every scene with Marilyn would be a painful marathon.

'She was awkward,' Stanwyck remembered. 'She couldn't get out of her own way. She wasn't disciplined, and she was often late, and she drove Bob Ryan, Paul Douglas and myself out of our minds . . . but she didn't do it viciously.' Ryan's recollection: 'It upsets everyone's timing when someone like Marilyn doesn't show up on schedule and then stumbles and stammers. Missy [Stanwyck] and Paul and I were furious, ready to tell her exactly how we felt, but we melted. She was so childish – almost angelic and innocent. Marilyn never deliberately did anything wrong and we realized she was oblivious.'

Made in the Fall of 1951 and released in June the following year, *Clash by Night* helped turn the Hollywood buzz about Marilyn into the national obsession it would shortly become. She made the cover of *Look* Magazine and got write-ups as 'the new blonde bombshell of Hollywood' (*New York News*), and 'a real acting threat to the season's screen blondes' (*New York Post*). She was now making $500 a week.

The nude calendar episode in March 1952 firmly placed Marilyn in the nation's fantasy life. It wasn't the photo itself – that wasn't published in

LOVE NEST, A 1951 COMEDY STARRING THE UPCOMING JUNE HAVER. (KOBAL COLLECTION)

MARILYN AS THE 'OTHER WOMAN' IN *LET'S MAKE IT LEGAL*. (NATIONAL FILM ARCHIVE, LONDON)

Playboy until a year and a half afterwards. It was the incredible idea that someone whose name people knew would do such a thing. Public nudity was then as strange a concept as a two-headed baby, and the nation was agog that someone who wanted to be a movie star would have posed nude and then almost boasted about it when the fact became known. ('Did you really have nothing on?' 'Not true. I had the radio on.') By refusing to express any regrets at all, despite the initial panic on the part of Fox's publicity staff, Marilyn showed that she was capable of creating a new category of public figure to which she alone would belong. The word 'superstar' was coined for the likes of Lillian Gish in the 1920s, but it has never applied so aptly to anyone as it does to Marilyn.

From then on, for the next ten years until she died, every move Marilyn made was recorded for the public. The capper to the brouhaha over the calendar and the simultaneous revelation that Marilyn's mother was a mental patient, was her romance with newly retired baseball star Joe DiMaggio, which began at the same time – Spring 1952. A sexier couple couldn't have been imagined. The crowd went wild.

Oh yes, Marilyn was making movies too. *We're Not Married* was a 1952 portmanteau film with five separate episodes, each with the same premise: a couple discovers they are not really married. In Marilyn's episode she uses her rediscovered maidenhood to win the Miss Mississippi contest and then remarry hubby David Wayne. *Don't Bother to Knock*, based on the Charlotte Armstrong novel *Mischief*, was a milestone; it was Marilyn's first leading role, and it was her first full-length dramatic role. She plays a babysitter fixated on Richard Widmark, a neighbour whose love for singer Anne Bancroft is unrequited. Marilyn thinks Widmark is her boyfriend who died in the war, and she blames the child she's babysitting when Widmark doesn't know what she's talking about. She threatens suicide but Widmark calms her.

By the time these movies came out in the summer of 1952, Marilyn's image had become far bigger than her accomplishments. She was turning into a nationwide byword without any major film credits. Fox still ranked her as just a promising starlet. The way the studio thought, Marilyn was a photo opportunity, not an actress in need of a vehicle. In Fox's view, a piece of slap and tickle couldn't become a star. It was glamour that sold movies, not sexiness. Fox was slow to understand that public appetites were changing and thus was slow to exploit Marilyn.

The early 1950s was a low period for Hollywood generally, as television proved to be not a novelty but a fundamental threat to the entire movie business. Fox in particular decided to concentrate its resources on responding to TV with CinemaScope. This wide-screen process was suited to the kind of costume drama spectacles that weren't available on the small screen, such as *The Robe* and *Demetrius and the Gladiators*. CinemaScope was almost a hindrance when used to shoot what finally became recognized as Marilyn's forte, sex comedies.

IN *CLASH BY NIGHT*, WITH KEITH ANDES. (NATIONAL FILM ARCHIVE, LONDON)

WITH KEITH ANDES. (KOBAL COLLECTION)

MARILYN AND JOE DIMAGGIO ON THE SET OF *MONKEY BUSINESS*. (KOBAL COLLECTION)

WITH DAVID WAYNE IN *WE'RE NOT MARRIED*. (KOBAL COLLECTION)

The pre-CinemaScope *Monkey Business* (released in September 1952) showed what Marilyn could do in this genre. Cary Grant plays a researcher seeking a youth formula, but one of his chimpanzees invents it first. Grant inadvertently takes it and regresses. Marilyn, fumble-fingered secretary to Grant's boss Charles Coburn, is sent to retrieve him. They frolic around town, notably on roller-skates and in a careering car. Eventually all the cast drink the youth formula except Marilyn, whose character is naturally on the childish side anyway. 'Half-child,' murmurs Grant. 'Not the visible half,' argues Grant's jealous wife, Ginger Rogers.

Making this jolly little movie in April 1952 was Marilyn's biggest professional challenge to date, and it almost broke her. The stress of suddenly achieving all the fame anyone could want put her in the hospital soon after production began. 'Appendicitis' was the story the studio put out, though no appendix was removed. With Cary Grant's agreement, director Howard Hawks revamped the film's shooting schedule to film her scenes last.

'Marilyn Monroe was the most frighened little girl, who had no confidence in her ability,' Hawks later said. 'She was afraid to come on the set. Very strange girl . . . but when she got out in front of the camera, the camera liked her, suddenly she was a great sex symbol. I was lucky to work with her early, before she became frightened . . . I had an easy time compared with other directors who worked with her later. The more important she became the more frightened she became.'

Of all the actors Marilyn worked with, Joseph Cotten gave the most indulgent portrait. He starred with her in *Niagara*, a psychological thriller made on location at Niagara Falls. *Niagara* came out in January 1953, after *O. Henry's Full House*. This 1952 release was another five-episode picture, in which Marilyn played a prostitute who frightens off two tramps (Charles Laughton and David Wayne).

Niagara is a Hitchcockish mood piece, complete with phallic tower and Freudian waterfall. Cotten, shell-shocked from the war, has brought Marilyn to Niagara Falls to try and rekindle her affection for him. She, however, is plotting with a new lover to kill him. Also at the motel overlooking the Falls are Jean Peters and her husband. Peters commiserates with Cotten when Marilyn dazzles everybody with a low-cut red dress: 'Cut down so low in front you can see her kneecaps,' as Cotten complains.

Marilyn and her shadowy lover arrange that a certain tune, 'Kiss Me', will be played on the town's bell tower as a signal that Cotten is dead. Cotten, however, discovers their scheme. When Marilyn hears the tune, she doesn't know that Cotten has turned the tables and that the body on the morgue table will be her lover. She tries to take a bus out of town but Cotten is lurking in the station. He follows her up the tower and strangles her under the silent bells: 'Too bad they can't play for you now, Rose.' Later, attempting to escape, Cotten vanishes over the Falls.

DON'T BOTHER TO KNOCK: MARILYN'S FIRST LEADING ROLE.

A PHOTO OPPORTUNITY WITH RICHARD WIDMARK.
(NATIONAL FILM ARCHIVE, LONDON)

WITH CARY GRANT IN *MONKEY BUSINESS*. (KOBAL COLLECTION)

MONKEY BUSINESS. (NATIONAL FILM ARCHIVE, LONDON)

WITH JOSEPH COTTEN IN *NIAGARA*. (NATIONAL FILM ARCHIVE, LONDON)

NIAGARA. (NATIONAL FILM ARCHIVE, LONDON)

AS ROSE LOOMIS IN *NIAGARA*. (NATIONAL FILM ARCHIVE, LONDON)

NIAGARA. (NATIONAL FILM ARCHIVE, LONDON)

Recalling the making of *Niagara*, Cotten described one pre-dinner cast get-together in his hotel room at the Falls. Marilyn arrived late 'as was her wont', wearing a white terrycloth robe and slippers she'd stolen from the Sherry Netherland Hotel in New York. '"Is this where the party is?" She came in and bestowed a velvety sensuous "Hi" on those assembled . . . and sat on the floor.'

Whereas she was 'outgiving and charming' and 'defensively shy' in such social settings, she was her familiar exasperating self when working. Cotten mentioned a phenomenon noted by others – Marilyn's tendency to lose concentration at any moment, even when the camera was rolling: 'Suddenly, her focus would move into outer space, thrusting her into a cloud of blankness.' Between shots, Marilyn was apt to complain about the studio's tight-fistedness: 'By the time I pay my dramatic coach, my singing teacher and my dancing master, there's hardly enough for my analyst.' She didn't like dealing with the production's schedulers, asking a minion at one point, 'Am I making a picture or punching a time clock?' She once dismissed director Henry Hathaway in Cotten's hearing: 'Go away, you annoy me.'

Such conflicts were to be repeated on a daily basis right to the end. Director after director found himself helpless with rage. The studio owned her but couldn't control her. Many of her co-stars felt they might as well be acting with a statue, and some felt worse than that; Tony Curtis went so far as to crack that 'Kissing Marilyn is like kissing Hitler'. The actors and directors who emerged least scarred after working with her were those who responded most wholeheartedly to the child inside her.

FOUR
'She got her life so balled up...'

JANE RUSSELL AS MARILYN IN *GENTLEMEN* . . .
(NATIONAL FILM ARCHIVE, LONDON)

*M*arilyn always yearned to be part of a family. She grew up the daughter of nobody in particular and was just as likely to sit down to dinner with strangers as with relations. She knew what families were supposed to be and she knew that she had missed out. Where love was concerned, she seemed most comfortable in relationships mimicking those found in a conventional family. She was less successful at creating equal male-female relationships – with other adults she tended to play the role of the baby or the little sister. Only with children was she able to assume full adult stature. All her life she attached herself to her friends' and associates' happy families, playing 'aunt' to their children for long periods. In her later years, she wanted desperately to become a mother herself, but the abortions she'd undergone earlier were the apparent cause of her several miscarriages.

If she was the child-woman that so many testify to, the child in her came out most strongly when she was make-believing – that is, acting. 'Oblivious', to use Robert Ryan's word, is the way a child playing with her dolls can sometimes appear. At work, Marilyn was in her own little world. She was unable to think of others' needs and afterwards would seem to forget why everybody was so mad at her. There was a certain state of mind that she had to attain before she could work properly, and until she reached it she would dawdle in her dressing-room – no matter how many people were being kept waiting.

The trouble was, when she was in this state of mind, that by the time she arrived at this feeling of oneness with the character she was playing, such mundane things as lines got crowded out of her head. She also had trouble hitting her marks, those little lines of tape on the floor placed to indicate where actors should stand to be in camera focus. Coordinating bits of business with movement and lines of dialogue was often beyond her.

From the beginning to the end of her career, she made long scenes exquisite torture for everyone she worked with. Dozens of takes were often required to shoot an acceptable 'master' (the version of a scene, always shot first, in which all the actors and the whole set are shown). Two-shots (scenes in which two actors appear on screen together) were maddening because most of what the other actor did went to waste. Marilyn blew her lines time after time, but her co-star could never coast because he or she never knew when Marilyn might get it right. In the cutting room, editors hunted for the takes in which Marilyn's magic came through, and if the other actor looked cross-eyed, too bad. The results of Marilyn's on-the-set struggles are often visible in her movies today. The cuts are sometimes quicker than the rhythm of a scene indicates, as the editor obviously searched among the close-ups for usable footage. Dialogue is sometimes heard and not seen, suggesting that not even post-syncing (dialogue recorded after shooting is completed) could correct the damage of dropped lines. Every film needs to be patched together, but Marilyn's needed more stitches than most.

MARILYN IN *GENTLEMEN PREFER BLONDES*. (KOBAL COLLECTION)

Marilyn's co-stars coped with her in varying ways. Those who came away least upset by the experience were those, like Jane Russell, who adapted their methods to hers. Russell found exactly the right relationship. During the making of *Gentlemen Prefer Blondes* in late 1952, she became Marilyn's big sister.

Aside from the same astrological sign (Gemini), they had something else in common – men who were prominent sports stars. Marilyn was in love with her baseball hero, Joe DiMaggio, and Russell had Bob Waterfield, one of the best quarterbacks in pro football. Both men were occasional visitors to the *Blondes*' set. 'Marilyn had a lot of questions to ask me about what it was like being married to an athlete,' Russell recalled. 'I told her, "Well, they're birds of a feather and you'll get to know lots of other athletes – otherwise it's great."'

The two actresses' relationship in the film is also something of a double date. They play showgirls bound for Paris on the *Île de France*, where Marilyn expects to marry her rich sweetheart, played by Tommy Noonan. Noonan's father hires a private eye (Elliott Reid) to spy on Marilyn. Russell and Reid fall in love. Marilyn, meanwhile, has her eye on a diamond merchant, Charles Coburn. Evidence of this dalliance stops Marilyn's wedding, and she and Russell get work in a nightclub. When Marilyn is accused of taking Coburn's wife's diamond tiara, Russell in a blonde wig impersonates Marilyn in court. It's a happy ending all around, with a double wedding. The movie was a big hit, and everyone left the cinemas humming Marilyn's show-stopper, 'Diamonds Are a Girl's Best Friend'. (This number, in which a stageful of male dancers dangle diamonds before her, helped inspire Madonna's lucrative impersonation of Marilyn thirty years later. The theme of Madonna's 'Material Girl' and its video recall this Marilyn signature tune.)

Jane Russell, a real trouper, suffered from none of Marilyn's in-securities but sympathized with her co-star's inability to cope. 'Baby Doll' was one of Russell's pet names for Marilyn. Russell diagnosed Marilyn's problem in simple terms – shyness and fear – and dealt with her in a friendly, no-nonsense way. When Marilyn stayed in her dressing-room too long, Russell recalled, 'I'd stand in her doorway and say, "C'mon, Blondie, let's go," and she'd say, "Oh! Okay," in her whispery voice, and we'd go on together.'

Marilyn felt most comfortable revealing her insecurities to the least threatening individual around her. At this time it was make-up man Whitey Snyder. Snyder had worked on *Niagara* and during shooting of that film had been entrusted with the duty of shepherding Marilyn to New York City when she rendez-voused with DiMaggio there. His duty now involved hours of having his ear bent by Marilyn's compulsive fretting. At this point, Marilyn's lateness wasn't the result of her drug problem. Troubled nights were not yet making her physically unable to work in the mornings. Snyder told Russell

'DIAMONDS ARE A GIRL'S BEST FRIEND'.
(KOBAL COLLECTION)

WITH JANE RUSSELL. (NATIONAL FILM
ARCHIVE, LONDON)

JANE RUSSELL AND MARILYN MONROE. (NATIONAL FILM ARCHIVE, LONDON)

that Marilyn had no problem arriving at the studio on time. Sitting for the first time in a star's vast dressing-room, Marilyn simply dwelt on her fears. Snyder said, 'I think she's afraid to go out.'

The hard work on preparation and rehearsal didn't bother Marilyn. Before *Gentlemen Prefer Blondes* went into production, she and Russell spent weeks blocking out their dance routines with choreographer Jack Cole and his assistant Gwen Verdon. Marilyn regularly worked with Cole for an hour or two after Russell went home. Cole told Russell that Marilyn needed those extra hours not to improve her dancing but to allay her insecurity.

The highly professional Russell described Marilyn as '. . . a dreamy girl. She's the kind liable to show up with one red shoe and one black shoe . . . I'd find out when we'd take a break at eleven that she hadn't had any breakfast and forgot she was hungry until I reminded her. Once she got her life so balled up that the studio hired a full-time secretary-maid for her. So Marilyn got the secretary as balled up as she was and she ended up waiting on the secretary instead of vice versa.'

Gentlemen Prefer Blondes director Howard Hawks was the first of several directors to clash point-blank with Marilyn's coach, Natasha Lytess. Lytess had remained close to Marilyn since meeting her at Columbia on *Ladies of the Chorus*. At one point she had moved in with her pupil, and according to one source their relationship had a sexual element. Marilyn's maid and confidante in later years, Lena Pepitone, claimed that Marilyn had told her, 'I let Natasha, but that was wrong.'

Whatever the truth of that, it is indisputable that throughout the early 1950s Marilyn couldn't make a move in front of a movie camera without seeing Lytess nod approval. In addition to working on her lines with Lytess the night before, Marilyn felt she needed Lytess's help on the set during the day as well. When Marilyn's dependence on her coach reached the point where she began ignoring the director, Hawks had Lytess barred from the set.

On every succeeding film Marilyn made, she fought to keep her coach – after Lytess it was Paula Strasberg – near her on the set at all times. Most of the men who directed her, except perhaps Joshua Logan and George Cukor, seemed unable to reconcile their need for control over their productions with her need to feel comfortable, no matter how long it took to reach that state. It is curious, though, how many of her directors came back for a second round with her – Howard Hawks, John Huston, Billy Wilder and Cukor.

Marilyn worked at the end of the era when pictures were directed from the top. In the 1950s, only a few actors, notably Burt Lancaster and Kirk Douglas, were able to control their productions. Women like Jane Fonda, Sally Field and Bette Midler routinely produce their own films now, but back then the slightest deviation by an actor from the front office's dictums brought a reprimand. Marilyn's insistence on the presence of a coach was a challenge to the studio system's hierarchical mind-set. Her lateness and lapses of concentration in front of the camera were ultimately far more harmful than her reliance on her coach. Fox and her directors couldn't do any more than wring their hands over the extra hours in her dressing-room and the wasted hours struggling to say her lines correctly. Lytess and later Strasberg, however, were easier targets for Marilyn's bosses' frustration. Bickering over this issue never stopped.

FIVE

'She had no meanness in her'

AS POLA DEBEVOISE, WITH DAVID WAYNE.
(NATIONAL FILM ARCHIVE, LONDON)

At Fox in the postwar years, the reigning blonde was Betty Grable. Her bathing suit pin-up had been a servicemen's favourite during the Second World War, and her fairly chaste brand of sex appeal seemed to define the limit of what could be shown on screen. Though it seemed inexplicable to Grable, a seasoned professional at the peak of her popularity, Fox began easing her out as soon as the studio recognized what it had in Marilyn Monroe. Grable herself knew the score: Alice Faye had been Fox's blonde until studio boss Darryl F. Zanuck brought in Grable in 1940.

Grable had originally been pencilled in for the role of Lorelei Lee in *Gentlemen Prefer Blondes* but saw the role go to her younger rival. When Fox embarked on the umpteenth remake of *How to Marry a Millionaire* in early 1953 and anticipation built over the forthcoming summer release of *Gentlemen Prefer Blondes*, Grable found herself in the humbling position of having to pass her crown on to Marilyn in public. As the story goes, the first time she and Marilyn worked together on the sound stage, Grable announced, 'I've had mine. Now go get yours.'

From the technical standpoint, *How to Marry a Millionaire* was a difficult project. It was only the second movie made in CinemaScope, and the first, *The Robe*, was a half-year away from release when *How to Marry a Millionaire* was shooting. Fox's camera experts were therefore still tinkering with the process.

Admirably suited to large vistas and biblical epics' casts of thousands, CinemaScope was less easily adapted to contemporary comedies set indoors with small casts. The CinemaScope screen was more than twice as wide as it was high. Therefore, in order to avoid leaving large patches of the screen empty, the director had to move the actors around constantly. Widescreen films avoid static shots and instead have longer, more fluid scenes.

The more successful the film-makers were in filling the CinemaScope screen, the less watchable their movies are today. Video versions show only the middle of what's meant to be shown, except when the movie is 'panned and scanned' or miniaturized into a horizontal bar across the middle third of the screen. During shooting, too, these technical exigencies didn't play to Marilyn's strongest suits, for she was not at her best trying to remember several pages of dialogue while hitting several different marks on a set. Another quirk of 'Scope was its tendency to fatten actors. Because of the process's highly horizontal aspect ratio, performers seemed to bulge toward the far-distant edges of the screen. This was not so bad for gladiators and gunslingers, but was trouble for actresses. Marilyn shed some weight to achieve greater verticality in such *How to Marry a Millionaire* scenes as the one in which she models a bathing suit.

The movie itself was yet another variation on one of Hollywood's longest-running themes: three girls go to the city seeking rich husbands. All of Busby Berkeley's 'Gold Diggers' musicals for Warners in the 1930s used that plot, and so had such Fox films as *Three Blind Mice* and *Three Little Girls*

HOW TO MARRY A MILLIONAIRE: THE BATHING SUIT SCENE.
(NATIONAL FILM ARCHIVE, LONDON)

in Blue. One of Grable's early Fox films was *Moon Over Miami* (1941), about two sisters seeking rich husbands. The most direct source for *How to Marry a Millionaire* was *The Greeks Had a Word for Them* (1932), later released as *Three Broadway Girls*. The enduring appeal of this retrograde scenario is perhaps Hollywood's best demonstration of where feminism is coming from.

Marilyn, Grable and Lauren Bacall play three husband-hunters named Pola Debevoise, Loco Dempsey and Schatze Page. They rent a penthouse in Manhattan, pretending they're well-off and hoping to attract well-heeled men. Marilyn's love interest is David Wayne, whom she 'meets cute' when she gets on the wrong plane. She boarded the wrong plane because she refused to wear her glasses in public. Wayne turns out to be her landlord, preoccupied by a dispute with the taxman.

Bacall is really the central character of the movie. It is she who rents the penthouse and hocks the furniture to support the girls' schemes, and she is the only one who actually marries a millionaire. Grable was top-billed on screen, though Marilyn dominated the advertising art. Grable's hair was bleached a truly arctic shade of blonde and it was to be the last time that Marilyn, quite platinum herself in the movie, was out-blonded on screen.

A neophyte beside Bacall and Grable, Marilyn lost out in the competition for screen time and the best lines, though she did get the most eye-catching and revealing costumes – mostly in bold hues like stark crimson or royal purple. Her character's mentality is dumb on dumb – 'foot in mouth' humour, as one critic admiringly called it.

Pola Debevoise is obsessed with the idea that she's unattractive in glasses – as well she might be, for the pair she does occasionally put on are two-toned, winged and unbecoming. No mistress of repartee, this character answers David Wayne's praise, 'I think you're quite a strudel', with merely, 'Honestly?' Marilyn's little sallies charmed the critics, such as Otis L. Guernsey Jr of the *New York Herald Tribune*, who gushed when the film opened in November, 'Her stint as a deadpan comedienne is as nifty as her looks . . . . [she has] a limpid guile that nearly melts the screen.' But her place in the order of things is defined in the dialogue, in such lines as Bacall's reference to her as 'Little Miss Bubblehead'.

Marilyn herself was no more prepossessing off camera than her ditsy character on screen. In Grable's and Bacall's testimony, their co-star was one of nature's lovable klutzes. They were professional enough to realize that she would never be professional. As Jane Russell did, they laughed off her exasperating bad habits and treated her like their retarded little sister.

Grable told two stories about Marilyn that sound shaggy-doggy – except that everyone told similar stories. There's a scene in the movie in which Marilyn appears barefoot. On the day that she shot the scene, Marilyn shuffled onto the soundstage with feet so filthy that a horrified Grable pulled her into her own dressing-room and washed her feet for her – and painted her toenails.

WITH BETTY GRABLE AND LAUREN BACALL.
(NATIONAL FILM ARCHIVE, LONDON)

Another time, Grable took responsibility for getting Marilyn to a studio banquet in one piece. In those days a studio could command all its contract players' attendance at such publicity functions. Grable, who had assured Marilyn's punctuality by craftily telling her the banquet started an hour earlier than it actually did, recalled Marilyn fussing with an elaborate pair of long white gloves. Marilyn liked the effect of the gloves so much that she kept them on during dinner, even while eating corn on the cob.

It was easy to laugh at Marilyn, from gentle ribbing to devastating scorn, depending upon your outlook on life. Grable liked to rib Marilyn by always demanding, 'Marilyn who?' when she called. The idea rarely entered Marilyn's head that other people weren't as serious about everything as she was.

Where men were concerned, Marilyn walked through a cloud of sexual innuendo. Before she was 'somebody', she used to dignify men's barbed remarks by whispering, 'Promises, promises'. Later, she either pretended not to hear them or was in such a fog she couldn't. Nunnally Johnson, writer-producer of *Gentlemen Prefer Blondes*, gave this scathing description of working with Marilyn: 'Monroe is something of a zombie. Talking to her is like talking to somebody under water – ten feet under water . . . You can't get through to her. She reminds me of a sloth. You stick a pin in a sloth's belly and eight days later it says "Ouch".'

Gerald Wiggins, a jazzman often hired in the 1950s to coach Marilyn's singing, recalled a different person: 'I'd meet her every day at the studio. She'd have the words down, and I'd just coach her on the tune, try to give her a few little jazz licks. She was a very good pupil, a pleasure to work with. She took care of business. She was no dumb blonde.' Of course, working with Wiggins, Marilyn didn't have to agonize over her hair and make-up or weigh the politics of every career-building move. Without the pressure of having to live up to the image she was building – who really cared whether she could sing? – Marilyn was able to do her work harmoniously and efficiently.

On the set, though, Marilyn's work habits were irritating. One particularly irksome habit Marilyn had was refusing to look into other actors' eyes when playing a scene with them. Bacall, like Grable, tried to be tolerant, recognizing this as a symptom of fright and insecurity, not disdain or standoffishness. Bacall bemoaned the fifteen or more takes a scene might take if Marilyn was in it.

'Marilyn was frightened, insecure – trusted only her coach and was always late. During our scenes she'd look at my forehead instead of my eyes; at the end of the take, look to her coach, standing behind [director] Jean Negulesco, for approval. If the headshake was no, she'd insist on another take. A scene often went to fifteen or more takes, which meant I'd have to be as good in all of them as no one knew which one would be used. Not easy – often irritating. And yet I couldn't dislike Marilyn. She had no meanness in

GRABLE, BACALL AND MONROE. (NATIONAL FILM ARCHIVE, LONDON)

BIG-TIME, GRAND-TIME ENTERTAINMENT IN

CINEMASCOPE

YOU
SEE IT
WITHOUT
THE USE OF
SPECIAL
GLASSES

20th Century-Fox presents

Marilyn MONROE · Betty GRABLE · Lauren BACALL
How To Marry A Millionaire

co-starring DAVID WAYNE · RORY CALHOUN · CAMERON MITCHELL with ALEX D'ARCY · FRED CLARK and William POWELL

Produced by NUNNALLY JOHNSON · Directed by JEAN NEGULESCO · Screen Play by NUNNALLY JOHNSON
Based on plays by Zoe Akins and Dale Eunson and Katherine Albert

COLOUR BY
TECHNICOLOR

(NATIONAL FILM ARCHIVE, LONDON)

her – no bitchery. She just had to concentrate on herself and the people who were only there for her.'

Bacall noted Marilyn's inability to connect in normal social give-and-take with those who weren't 'only there for her'. 'There was something sad about her – wanting to reach out – afraid to trust – uncomfortable.' At this time Marilyn was in love with DiMaggio and kept trying to imagine herself as a wife and mother like Bacall, who was Mrs Humphrey Bogart. In fantasizing a domestic life for herself, Marilyn apparently summoned all the realism of a child playing with dolls. Bacall remembered, 'She seemed envious of that aspect of my life – wistful – hoping to have it herself one day . . . I think she did trust me and like me as well as she could anyone whose life must have seemed to her so secure, so solved.'

Director Jean Negulesco joined most of her directors in saying that, after all was said and done, it didn't matter how unpleasant it was to work with Marilyn. 'In the end I adored her, because she was a pure child who had this "something" that God had given her, that we still can't define or understand. It's the thing that made her a star. We did not know whether she'd been good or bad, and then when we put the picture together, there was one person on the screen who was a great actress – Marilyn.'

SIX
'A really great dame'

WITH ROBERT MITCHUM IN *RIVER OF NO RETURN*.
(NATIONAL FILM ARCHIVE, LONDON)

Robert Mitchum and Marilyn Monroe were two of a kind: each excelled when no one else was on the screen. Wooden-faced Bob never could make a romantic relationship believable, and Marilyn hardly ever played two-scenes successfully unless she was at cross-purposes with her leading man. Mitchum himself said, 'Marilyn and I are a lot alike. There's not one single day when we can do one single thing completely gracefully. We're always in the soup.'

The standard plot of a Monroe movie presents her as an unattainable beauty who can't grasp the needs of the man who's after her. And her character is often an entertainer or professional beauty of some kind, further distancing her from the mere mortal who admires her. The more artificial the set-up, the more misunderstandings it generated, the better Marilyn was.

Which brings us to *River of No Return*, a mismatch from the start. Marilyn, who wore glamorous costumes better than anyone before or since, spends much of the movie in jeans. Whereas she worked most effectively with mild, unthreatening citified leading men, here she had hulking out-door man Mitchum. Most comfortable in a studio under controlled lighting, she was now in the great northern woods of Canada. And never very happy with control-minded directors, she drew Hollywood's most fanatical disci-plinarian, Otto Preminger, whose favourite pastime was humiliating actresses in front of everyone.

Notwithstanding all these negatives, *River of No Return* was an import-ant step up the ladder for Marilyn. For the first time, the audience wasn't shielded from Marilyn's blatant sexuality by the presence of a more promi-nent, more circumspect, and older female co-star. She sang more solos (four) than ever before – deathless Ken Darby–Lionel Newman tunes like 'I'm Gonna File My Claim'.

The confused plot of *River* has Marilyn roaming the West in 1875, singing in saloons and consorting with gamblers. Mitchum, just out of prison, has a ten-year-old son whose mother is dead. Man and boy set off for a life of sodbusting. Marilyn pops up in distress on a raft in the swift river running by Mitchum's farm. With her is cardsharp Rory Calhoun. No sooner is Calhoun rescued than he steals Mitchum's horse just when the Indians are about to attack. Mitchum and son and Marilyn take the raft to town. The task of shooting down Calhoun is left to the boy.

Director Preminger was as miscast on this picture as the leading lady. The Viennese autocrat's forte was realistic character dramas like *Stalag 17* and *Anatomy of a Murder*, not Western fantasies with music. But Preminger's contract with Fox required him to accede to Zanuck's fiat that he and only he should direct Monroe 'out West'. Possibly the studio boss (whose biography by Mel Gussow was aptly titled *Don't Say Yes Until I Finish Talking*) thought Preminger could control Marilyn's excesses.

Preminger couldn't. *River* was the first time Marilyn used her box-office power to show who was really in charge on the set. It's curious that

RIVER OF NO RETURN, WITH ROBERT MITCHUM.
(NATIONAL FILM ARCHIVE, LONDON)

someone with so fragile an ego as Marilyn's should wind up making strong men cry. But from here on, until her addictions led her to overplay her hand just before her death, Marilyn knew she didn't really have to listen to what anybody said.

They say movies are 'a collaborative art', and maybe that characterization has some validity today, when the business is less monolithic and more professionalized than it was in the 1950s. In those days heads of studios exercised power nakedly through iron-clad contracts and through volcanic force of personality. Stars sometimes objected and even rebelled; depending on their importance, they were placated or crushed. Since Chaplin, Fairbanks, Griffith and Pickford had formed United Artists in 1919, it wasn't until 1948 that another actor, Burt Lancaster, successfully created a structure to produce his own films. Marilyn was to become one of those who followed Lancaster in forming her own production company in 1955. But in 1953 her aims were more tactical than strategic – she didn't want to take direction from the dictatorial Preminger.

Preminger, for whom no actress was ever good enough, constantly insulted Marilyn on the set. Shelley Winters made a pilgrimage to the Canadian location in August and recalled, 'Preminger began to use dreadful language, implying that she was so untalented that she should stick to her original "profession".' Preminger campaigned to 'naturalize' Marilyn's over-rehearsed, stagey way of walking and talking. Everything that had worked for Marilyn in deliberately artificial movies like *Gentlemen Prefer Blondes* was supposed to be forgotten now that she was playing a Wild West *chanteuse*.

Mitchum recalled seeing Preminger demonstrate to Marilyn how he wanted her to walk. The sight of the tubby, bald director mincing around the set would have been amusing if the conflict hadn't been of the utmost importance to the combatants. Marilyn won this battle by contriving to hurt her ankle while trying to do it Preminger's way.

Next Preminger attacked Marilyn's accent. In most of Marilyn's films she over-enunciates, like a bright kewpie doll. That's part of her charm as a comedienne. But her 'A in elocution' style of speech was less successful in drama. What made the problem so maddening to Preminger was that her natural way of speaking was exactly what he needed on screen and couldn't get.

In Preminger's view, 'Marilyn's ambition was to become a great dramatic actress. She underrated her natural magic in front of the camera. As a result she always employed a coach . . . Marilyn clung to these coaches and accepted blindly any advice they gave her, most of which was bad.'

Natasha Lytess got Preminger's goat from day one, when the cast and crew of the film company embarked from Los Angeles on a special train to the film's location near Banff, British Columbia, in the Canadian Rockies. Along for the ride were DiMaggio and a friend of his, a ticket broker named

OTTO PREMINGER. (NATIONAL FILM ARCHIVE, LONDON)

Georgie Solotaire. It was in the dining car that Preminger, an Austrian, saw through Lytess's pretence of being Russian. 'She was in fact German,' he sniffed.

'Natasha had a theory that Marilyn shouldn't speak in the soft, slurred voice that was so much a part of the unique image she projected on the screen. She wanted her to enunciate every syllable distinctly. Marilyn didn't question Natasha's judgement. She rehearsed her lines with such grave ar-tic-yew-lay-shun that her violent lip movements made it impossible to photograph her. Natasha applauded her on her marvellous pronunciation, which inspired Marilyn to exaggerate even more. I pleaded with her to relax and speak naturally but she paid no attention. She listened only to Natasha.'

Preminger had to be content with only small victories. As he recalled it, 'Robert Mitchum saved the situation. During rehearsals he ignored her studied affectation. Then, just as I was ready to shoot, he would slap her sharply on the bottom and snap, "Now stop that nonsense. Let's play it like human beings. Come on!" He managed to startle her and she dropped, at least for the moment, her Lytess mannerisms.'

For some reason, Marilyn wasn't happy to be spanked like a performing dog. When Preminger went to the length of barring Lytess from the set ('You can be with Miss Monroe in her dressing-room if she wants you there, but you are not permitted on the set,' Preminger told Lytess), Marilyn threatened to quit the picture. Her telegram to Zanuck brought a response from the studio that ordered Preminger to give Marilyn what she wanted. 'I had no choice but to give in,' Preminger lamented.

Lateness was another familiar point of conflict. Again Marilyn's inability to mind the clock infuriated her director, and again she got away with it. Preminger could only fume, 'It's okay for a star to be late, one time, two times. But fifty-four to fifty-six times is too much. It is beneath the dignity of any director to have to endure this.' But endure it he did.

Mitchum, who always approaches acting with an absence of fuss and feathers, has recalled only the lighter side of working with Marilyn. Telling scatological (and probably apocryphal) anecdotes is Mitchum's favourite way of passing the time. He has often told of his pre-war days as a sheet-metal worker at the Lockheed plant in Burbank where Marilyn's first husband James Dougherty also worked. Mitchum says Dougherty used to open his wallet and show off a snapshot of Marilyn wearing nothing but a short apron. Dougherty has said he never had such a snapshot.

Mitchum tells of standing around on the *River of No Return* set with Marilyn and his stand-in, when she remarked, 'What a set! A girl doesn't get much action around here.'

'My stand-in piped up, "What about a round robin." Marilyn didn't know what that was. "You and me and Mitchum," he said.

"Ooooh, that would kill me."

"Nobody's died from it yet."

"I bet they have. But in the papers it says the girl died from natural causes."'

Without going into his opinion of Marilyn's ar-tic-yew-lay-shun, Mitchum has recalled trying to film a love scene while she was exaggerating her lip movements in order to speak very clearly. He complained, 'How can I take aim when she's undulating that way?'

Mitchum's stories tend to improve with each telling. He remembers a moment of high adventure on the *River of No Return* set when he, Marilyn and young Tommy Rettig were on the raft and in danger of being swept downriver to a waterfall. A small rescue boat was dispatched to save the cast. Marilyn and the boy clambered in, but the boat seemed too small for Mitchum. Marilyn insisted that Mitchum be taken too, saying, 'He wouldn't be here if it weren't for me having to do the scene over.' Mitchum's verdict: 'Any girl with that much guts, I think, is a really great dame.'

SEVEN
'Big breasts, big ass, big deal'

MARRIAGE TO JOE DIMAGGIO, 1954. (POPPERFOTO)

*U*nquestionably Fox's biggest star after she finished *River of No Return*, and *How to Marry a Millionaire* opened in November 1953, Marilyn discovered that she had options. Instead of fighting for roles, she had to fight against them. She had to work less often and work at the top of the bills of the top films. Soon she would be talking about seeking strong dramatic roles, but for now she concentrated on trying to avoid sideways and backwards steps into too-dumb and too-small parts.

Fox wanted her virtually to repeat her *River of No Return* role in another picture about a performer in the Old West. It was a project called *Pink Tights*, and was to co-star Frank Sinatra, who had not yet won his Oscar for *From Here to Eternity*. The picture was to begin shooting at the start of 1954, but Marilyn refused the assignment. (Paramount shot the script five years later as *Heller in Pink Tights*, with Sophia Loren and Anthony Quinn.)

When Marilyn vetoed *Pink Tights*, Fox followed the usual Hollywood procedure with recalcitrant performers – it put her 'on suspension'. Suspension was both a punishment and a negotiating ploy. By keeping the performer's contract in force instead of cancelling it over the performer's alleged breach, a studio suspending an actor retained its control over his or her career. The length of time that the actor held out against the studio's wishes was simply added on to the end of the contract.

In challenging the studio this first time, Marilyn didn't have a case in law, but it's easy to sympathize with her complaints. She was earning $1500 a month at a time when the studio was making millions from her pictures. Jane Russell got six times Marilyn's salary for *Gentlemen Prefer Blondes*. The worst part of the contract was its requirement that she take whatever role the studio dished out, directed by whomever the studio chose.

Photographer Milton Greene helped show Marilyn a way out. Greene took his first pictures of Marilyn in mid-1953, shortly before she bowed out of *Pink Tights*. In January 1955 they were to join in creating Marilyn Monroe Productions, Marilyn's declaration of full independence.

At this point, though, in the spring of 1954, Marilyn demanded only partial autonomy. She compromised with Fox. If the studio would give her *The Seven Year Itch* she would make *There's No Business Like Show Business* and accept billing after Ethel Merman. She knew that with the Merman picture her career would be marking time at best, but the deal offered her an honourable way out of the contract suspension impasse. She wound up making *There's No Business Like Show Business* and *The Seven Year Itch* back to back in the summer and autumn of 1954.

Marilyn's off-screen life at this time also revolved around a too-binding contract – her marriage to DiMaggio on 14 January 1954. Studio publicity chief Harry Brand acknowledged the suspended star's marriage with the crack, 'We're not losing a star, we're gaining an outfielder.' The 286-day union was marked by Joltin' Joe's frequent protests that his wife, America's number one sex symbol, was doing her job too well. He was jealous (with

WITH DONALD O'CONNOR IN *THERE'S NO BUSINESS* . . . (NATIONAL FILM ARCHIVE, LONDON)

'LAZY' – WITH DONALD O'CONNOR AND MITZI GAYNOR. (NATIONAL FILM ARCHIVE, LONDON)

cause) and complained about her revealing costumes. (Marilyn rarely played nuns.) She wavered between trying to be the traditional homebody DiMaggio demanded and revelling in her ability to arouse men. When Marilyn was in trouble at the studio, she found that DiMaggio, not one of nature's hand-holders, wasn't equipped to provide the kind of support that she needed. She complained publicly that they were sleeping apart. He visited the set of *There's No Business Like Show Business* just once, and even then was generally heard complaining about the skimpiness of his wife's costume.

As artificial and contrived as the plot of *There's No Business Like Show Business* is, several scenes in the musical accurately mirror what was going on off camera. In the film, Marilyn plays a hat-check girl who rises to become a Broadway headliner. Like Marilyn, Vicki has problems with her articulation, has a yen to play the Russian classics, deals with a jealous boyfriend and argues at length over what costume to wear. Vicki says, 'I've been on my own since I was fifteen,' which Marilyn might have said herself. Vicki also speaks for Marilyn when she says, 'I want to show him I'm an actress too.' The agent who asks her, 'Will you forget that elocution stuff?' could have been listening to Otto Preminger. Marilyn even prefigures her own future switch in allegiance from Natasha Lytess to the Strasbergs in Vicki's line, 'I have a new manager and he's doing me over completely.' There's no business where art mirrors life like show business.

There's No Business Like Show Business was concocted for the movies out of Irving Berlin tunes cannibalized from his hits over the years. It's about two generations of the Donahue family, a vaudeville song and dance act headed by Merman and her husband, Dan Dailey. One of their sons, Donald O'Connor, happens to catch Marilyn's act. She steps out from behind the hat-check counter to slither from table to table singing a vampy 'After You Get What You Want, You Don't Want It'. O'Connor tries to con her by pretending to be a reporter, but she only has eyes for the producer who can advance her career.

Some time later, he has indeed advanced her career and she's sharing a bill with the Donahues. She rehearses 'Heat Wave', which turns out to be the Donahues' show-stopper. O'Connor lets her have the number. Climbing still further up the ladder, Marilyn becomes a headliner doing a hot triple-act with O'Connor and his sister Mitzi Gaynor. Marilyn is all breasts and buttocks in black toreador pants and leotard shirt with a deep-scooped neckline, singing 'Lazy' – 'Physically I'm in pretty good shape but mentally I'm comatose' – as she crawls and stretches over a divan. In the end, Marilyn has climbed to the very top – she's in the thirty-fourth week of her own revue on Broadway. She and O'Connor finally connect and she joins all the Donahues on stage singing the title number (which Merman had made famous on Broadway in *Annie Get Your Gun*).

In the two films Marilyn made in 1954, her annoying unprofessionalism

SINGING 'HEAT WAVE'. (NATIONAL FILM ARCHIVE, LONDON)

began to deteriorate into dangerous self-destructiveness. Now that the stakes had been raised, and more and more depended on her, it took more patience than most men had to chivvy her and kid her into putting her performance on film. At one point during the filming of *There's No Business Like Show Business* she repeatedly forgot a line that spoiled a lengthy take. She retreated in tears to her dressing-room and later emerged to apologize. She told costume designer Bill Travilla, 'You know, I'm losing a piece of my mind each day. My brains are leaving me. I think I'm going crazy, and I don't want to be seen this way. If I go crazy, please take me away and hide me.'

The person least equipped to sympathize with Marilyn's vagaries was salty old trouper Ethel Merman, who had starred on Broadway for decades. On the stage, Merman had never had to defer to the actress playing the ingenue, but in Hollywood she had less clout.

Until the last reel, Merman was hardly on screen with Marilyn, so she escaped most of the frustrations of working with her. On other occasions when they might have conflicted, Marilyn absented herself. One was a meet-the-cast party to which producer Sol Siegel invited all the featured players. Marilyn didn't show. Another was a stills session for the headliners. Again, Marilyn stayed away. A space was left in the group portrait; Marilyn would later pose alone and her photo would be superimposed in the gap.

Billing was a point of contention. Merman's deal was for 'first among equals' billing: no one's name would be more prominent than hers, and hers would come first. When the studio published the cast group photo in a trade paper, the caption unaccountably listed Marilyn first, followed by Dan Dailey and then Merman. Although Merman had conceded, 'Hell, she's the one we need to sell this picture', she wasn't willing to have her thunder stolen by someone half her age and with a tenth her professionalism. Thereafter all billing was according to contract.

Mitzi Gaynor recalled helping avert a potential Merman explosion: 'Whenever Marilyn wouldn't come out of her dressing-room, I gave Ethel a wink, hinting that something naughty was going on there. Of course, that wasn't true, but if Ethel thought maybe some hanky-panky was going on, she could enjoy the situation.'

Marilyn was in a position to influence how she was clothed and choreographed on screen, and she exercised her new power. 'At that point the studio was doing its goldarndest to keep her happy,' Merman recalled. Marilyn requested that Bill Travilla design her costumes instead of Miles White. She wanted Jack Cole to choreograph her 'Heat Wave' number instead of the man who arranged the rest of the picture's dances, Robert Alton. Alton's choreography for the number was too tame for Marilyn, who saw the number not as a plot point but as a chance to show her unique abilities. She said she 'wanted more movement in it'. In Dan Dailey's words, 'She wanted everything goin'.' Cole, who had choreographed Marilyn in

RESTING FROM *THERE'S NO BUSINESS* . . . WITH MITZI GAYNOR AND ETHEL MERMAN. (KOBAL COLLECTION)

ETHEL MERMAN, DAN DAILEY, MITZI GAYNOR, DONALD O'CONNOR AND MARILYN IN THE 'HEAT WAVE' SCENE. (NATIONAL FILM ARCHIVE, LONDON)

Gentlemen Prefer Blondes, conceived a super-slinky number in which she enters on a platform carried by four male dancers.

One point Marilyn didn't win was her wish to wear high heels in scenes with her love interest, Donald O'Connor. The boyish O'Connor wasn't Marilyn's idea of dream casting anyway. She told producer Siegel that O'Connor looked so young she could be his mother. Marilyn yielded to reason; she shed her heels to avoid looking gargantuan beside O'Connor.

In addition, there were all the usual conflicts with the film's director, Walter Lang. As Merman saw it, Marilyn took her direction instead from Lytess. Johnny Ray, who plays another of Merman's sons, once heard Lytess directing Marilyn, 'In this scene you are a bubble, and you float.' All the old pros on the set could only commiserate with bitter laughter at what they saw as Marilyn's antics. They weren't sympathetic at all when Marilyn called in sick three times, only angry that their schedules had to be revised. At the end, Marilyn and everybody else had to work straight through without days off to finish the picture.

An unhappy experience from start to finish, *There's No Business Like Show Business* appropriately enough turned out to be a disappointment at the box office. Marilyn's epitaph on the picture: 'I did what they said. And all it got me was a lot of abuse . . . Big breasts, big ass, big deal. Can't I be anything else?'

EIGHT
'Did I do all right?'

SHOOTING THE SUBWAY GRATING SCENE ON LEXINGTON AVENUE. (NATIONAL FILM ARCHIVE, LONDON)

*W*ithout a day's rest after *There's No Business Like Show Business* wrapped in August 1954, Marilyn went into *The Seven Year Itch*. This was another project based on Broadway-proven material – the hit play was still running in New York after two years – but one more suited to Marilyn's talents.

What were her talents? Marilyn arrived at the end of the period when song and dance and glamour and sexiness and comedy all seemed to belong together. To tie up such packages, the movies looked to Broadway for inspiration. But many of the younger musical comedy headliners like Gwen Verdon and Chita Rivera lacked whatever it is the camera loves, and their names weren't well known west of the Hudson River. So Hollywood usually gave their roles to better-known, less-talented stars – Natalie Wood, Kim Novak, Doris Day and, yes, Marilyn Monroe.

Fox floundered around for several years without giving Marilyn a role that would justify the extraordinary public interest in her. Marilyn could carry a tune, but not far. She could move, but not dance. She wouldn't have lasted a minute on stage. She wasn't designed to be seen from afar and heard up in the top balcony. Yet the studio kept trying to squeeze her into song-and-dance roles that either came from Broadway or were conceived in Broadway terms.

Marilyn's appearance made it hard for anybody in the 1950s to imagine her as part of anyone's ordinary experience. That's one reason she kept playing entertainers (another was to keep her sexiness safely distanced). Her characters can't help but exude artificiality. But at her best she combines her calculated effects with apparent unawareness of her effects. This touch-me-don't-touch-me tension is the essence of her appeal. That's why, when her character says something sexy, it's funny. She can be blatant because she doesn't know what she's saying.

So Marilyn shouldn't play a knowing character. She shouldn't calculate unless the audience knows her calculations are off-base. She needs the audience's full sympathy to have her proper effect. Men in the audience need to feel she needs protection, and women need to feel that the men sitting beside them see her as only a fantasy. She can play dramatic moments, but they'd better not be prolonged.

The above precisely describes Marilyn's unnamed character in Billy Wilder's *The Seven Year Itch*, the film that cemented Marilyn's image and proved that she was more than just a press agent's creation. Except for *The Misfits*, all of the roles she played afterwards also fitted into this framework. She and her agent, Charles K. Feldman, knew what they were doing when they negotiated the compromise with Fox that ensured Marilyn's casting in Wilder's film. Feldman had an independent axe to grind – he got an associate producer credit on the film. This well-paid perk was negotiated for him by Irving 'Swifty' Lazar, also the agent of Wilder and the film's writer George Axelrod. It was an early example of the agency packaging through

THE SEVEN YEAR ITCH, WITH TOM EWELL. (NATIONAL FILM ARCHIVE, LONDON)

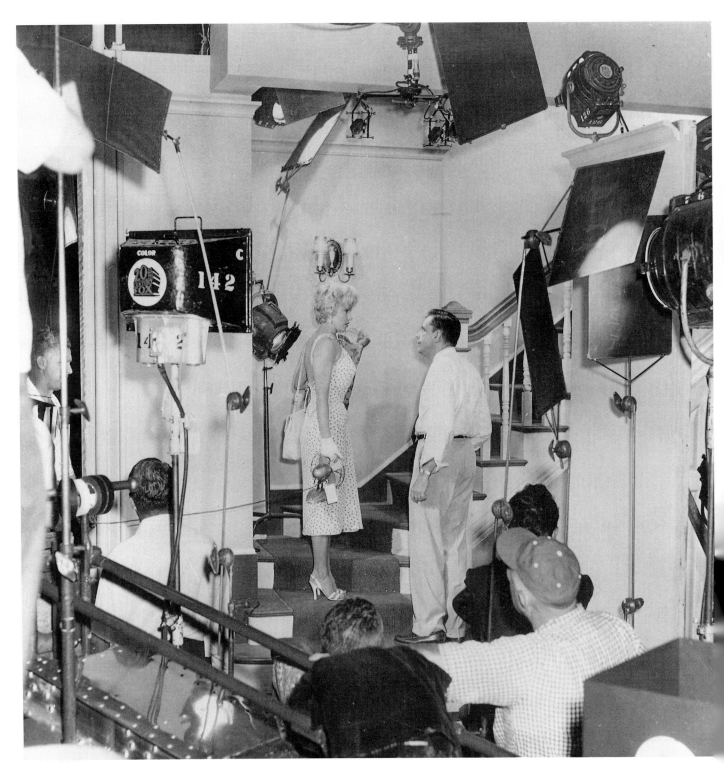

THE SEVEN YEAR ITCH. (NATIONAL FILM ARCHIVE, LONDON)

which so many films are made today. Such deals smell like roses when they result in hits like *Itch*, Fox's top grosser for 1955.

The Axelrod play, which had starred Tom Ewell and Vanessa Brown, is an early critique of 1950s innocence. A spoof of buttoned-down conformism, it's full of topical jokes and digs at psychology. Ewell plays a white-collar Manhattan apartment-dweller whose wife is spending the long, hot summer in the country. Alone with his fantasies, he discovers the beautiful model who lives upstairs, an innocent dingbat who declares, 'When it's hot like this, you know what I do? I keep my undies in the icebox!' Ewell soon imagines her unable to resist his advances. However, when she really does kiss him, it's merely to demonstrate the 'kissing sweet' chewing gum she plugs on TV. She tells him how she had to call the plumber when her toe got stuck in the faucet while she was taking a bath – occasioning yet another Ewell fantasy.

Their relationship advances from cocktails at his place to dinner and a film. On their way home, Marilyn's white skirt is blown up above her knees when she walks over a subway grate, and instead of being embarrassed she revels in the flow of air. The heat is such that when they return to Ewell's apartment, she proposes staying over to enjoy his air-conditioning. Of course, Ewell sleeps on the couch. 'You know what?' Marilyn pipes up innocently. 'We can do this all summer!' But all good things, however frustrating, must come to an end. Ewell has been imagining his wife having an affair with another man. When this fellow appears in his apartment, Ewell can't resist hinting the truth about his own would-be philandering. He refers to 'the blonde in the kitchen', and the other man asks, 'What blonde in the kitchen?' Ewell brings the house down by saying, 'Wouldn't you like to know – maybe it's Marilyn Monroe!' Mild kiss, curtain.

Ewell's 'Marilyn Monroe' joke perfectly encapsulates the self-referential appeal of *The Seven Year Itch*. Everybody who went to see the movie knew that Marilyn was more famous for being Marilyn than she was for being an actress. Few pictures received so much publicity during production. Two 'news' developments drew the most ink: Marilyn on location in New York shooting the subway grate scene; and Marilyn in Hollywood divorcing Joe DiMaggio.

The circus at 2 am on that late summer night on Lexington Avenue (under which the East Side IRT subway line runs) was a shrewdly executed publicity coup. The scene could have been shot on the q.t., but the studio tipped off the press in advance. A crowd estimated at four thousand pressed forward behind police barriers. As usual with any scene involving Marilyn, multiple re-takes were required until dawn terminated shooting. The story is told that Marilyn said to Wilder, 'I hope this isn't for your private collection, to be shown in stag shows.' Joe DiMaggio turned up at this exhibition of his wife's carnality, expressed his disgust to columnist Walter Winchell and left without speaking to Marilyn. These events were dramatized somewhat fancifully in the 1985 Nicolas Roeg film, *Insignificance*, starring Theresa Russell and Gary Busey as the Marilyn Monroe and Joe DiMaggio figures.

The humdrum footnote to the sensational location shoot was that none of the subway grating footage was actually used in the film. The footage of Marilyn's skirt billowing up was actually shot back at the studio, where the air currents and lighting could be better controlled.

But the stunt worked. The well-documented hot night on Lexington Avenue legitimized the wide circulation and publication of perhaps the most famous still in Hollywood history. This photograph, somewhat racier than the fleeting and quite modest glimpse of thigh shown in the film, was seen everywhere in the months leading up to the film's premiere the following June. In the years since, the still has become part of the movies' iconography. Ever afterwards, directors have occasionally steered starlets over air sources for a little skirt-billowing in the night. Ken Russell gave the scene its most memorable tribute in *Tommy*, when in a fantasy sequence he filled the screen with an army of life-sized sculptures modelled on the still.

Marilyn's break-up with Joe DiMaggio was also conducted in public. His version of events has never been told. Hers emphasizes his jealousy, aloofness and inflexibility. It was a marriage that was happier before it happened. It was over by 5 October 1954, when Marilyn called in and told Wilder she was taking the day off because she was getting a divorce. She obtained it officially on 27 October, on grounds of 'mental cruelty', a standard reason at the time. The studio called it a 'conflict of careers'.

Seeking solace ever more frequently in liquor and pills, increasingly doubtful of her abilities, and ever-aware that this film could be her route to the very top, Marilyn often disrupted *Itch*'s schedule. Because of her absences and her inability to work quickly when she was present, the film's cost rose $150,000 over budget to $1.8 million, a great deal for a production that was essentially a one-set, two-actor affair.

'She was never on time once,' recalled Billy Wilder, whose attitude towards Marilyn veered between exasperation and resignation. 'It is a terrible thing for an acting company, the director, the cameraman. You sit there and wait. You can't start without her. Thousands of dollars you see going into the hole. You can always figure a Monroe picture runs an extra few hundred thousand because she's coming later. It demoralizes the whole company. It's like trench warfare. You sit and sit, waiting for something to happen. When are the shells going to explode? On the other hand, I have an Aunt Ida in Vienna who is always on time, but I wouldn't put her in a movie.'

Wilder couldn't stay angry. His sense of humour kept saving him. He told a story illustrating how he saw Marilyn: 'Once when my car was in overhaul she gave me a lift from Fox to my house. She is driving this black Cadillac of hers. She received it from Jack Benny. She was a guest on his TV programme and this was her salary. I looked in the back of the car. Such a mess you wouldn't believe. It is like she threw everything in the back helter-

MARILYN WITH HER ATTORNEY FACING REPORTERS FOR THE FIRST TIME SINCE THE BREAK-UP OF HER MARRIAGE WITH JOE DIMAGGIO. (POPPERFOTO)

skelter because there's an invasion and the enemy is already in Pasadena. There's blouses lying there, and slacks, girdles, skirts, shoes, old plane tickets, old lovers for all I know – you never saw such a filthy mess in all your life. On top of the mess is a whole bunch of parking tickets.'

You couldn't stay mad at Marilyn. You had to love her. At the end of a scene she was capable of asking Wilder, like some beginning child actress, 'Did I do all right?' She would sit with the rest of the cast and crew watching 'rushes' of the previous day's shots. Instead of analysing and assessing her performance she would repeat it, with words and movement. The joke was that it was the only time she was sure to get her lines right. When the film finally wrapped, three weeks late, Marilyn remained on form, according to George Axelrod: 'Billy's a wonderful director. I want him to direct me again. But he's doing the Lindbergh story next. And he won't let me play Lindbergh.'

NINE
'I'm tired of sex roles'

BUS STOP, WITH DON MURRAY. (KOBAL COLLECTION)

Whatever her contract said, Marilyn felt she had completed her obligation to Fox. At Zanuck's insistence, she had made a turkey (*There's No Business Like Show Business*), and in return he had permitted her to give the studio a hit (*The Seven Year Itch*). On the evidence, who knew better – she or Zanuck – which films she should do? So with the help of Milton Greene, she plotted her declaration of independence from the studio. They figured that the time was right for her to rebel, for she would never have more leverage than just after completing a sure-fire smash.

Marilyn, the world's worst employee, had three quarrels with Fox. First, she wanted her pay to relate more closely to her value to the studio. Second, she wanted more control over the roles she played. Third, she wanted director approval. The way to reach these goals, she decided under Greene's influence, was to do nothing until Fox gave her a new contract. She determined to emphasize the seriousness of her position by leaving Hollywood and going to New York.

Always responsive to men who praised her for qualities other than her looks, Marilyn not only moved to New York at the end of 1954, she moved in with Greene and his family. She spent Christmas in Connecticut with Greene, his wife and their baby. Early in 1955, as *There's No Business Like Show Business* was opening poorly, she held her decisive press conference.

'A new woman' in her own estimation, Marilyn said, 'I'm tired of sex roles. I'm going to broaden my scope. People have scope, you know . . . they really do.' She said she 'didn't like a lot of my pictures'. In order to make pictures she did like, she was forming Marilyn Monroe Productions, of which she would own fifty-one per cent (according to Arthur Miller, Marilyn had a lengthy battle of wills with Greene before obtaining this majority share of herself). A few months after her press conference, she went on Edward R. Murrow's *Person to Person* chat show and said, 'It's not that I object to doing musicals or comedy – in fact, I rather enjoy it – I'd like to do dramatic parts too.'

The studio fought back. Just as Grable had replaced Alice Faye and Marilyn had replaced Grable, Sheree North was brought in to replace the recalcitrant Marilyn. Hoping to do business at the same old stand, Fox was producing another 'how-to' picture – *How to Be Very, Very Popular* – which was to be Grable's last hurrah. Fox had wanted Marilyn to re-team with Grable in this film, a re-make of a re-make, but Marilyn felt she shouldn't go back to playing shallow sexpots in conventional glamour pictures. She felt that after *Itch* she needn't share the screen with another blonde – or with any other actress, in fact.

A former dancer, North's job in *How to Be Very, Very Popular* was to be the sexy ingenue, but something was missing. Despite all the publicity the studio could plant, the film did poorly. So did several other North vehicles made during the year Marilyn was in New York. The failure of the Sheree

WITH MILTON GREENE. (KOBAL COLLECTION)

North ploy and the great popularity of *The Seven Year Itch* forced Fox to negotiate with Marilyn.

Fox premiered *Itch* in New York on Marilyn's twenty-ninth birthday, 1 June 1955. Marilyn ensured blanket coverage of the event by stepping out of the limousine with Joe DiMaggio, of all people. After all, she couldn't be seen yet with her new lover, Arthur Miller. When Miller had met Marilyn on a Fox sound stage in 1950, the playwright recalled in his autobiography *Timebends*, he had found her 'almost ludicrously provocative', but he had contented himself with a kiss on the cheek and had gone back to his wife in New York. Now, with Marilyn living in the Waldorf Towers on East 50th Street while he attended rehearsals of his play *A View from the Bridge* at the New Amsterdam roof theatre on 42nd Street, Miller embarked on the affair he had resisted five years before. As he hurried through the lobby of the theatre to Marilyn's bed, he would pass a life-size cut-out photo of her.

The reviews of *Itch* reflected the hedonist-Puritan division in American attitudes towards Marilyn. 'This is the picture every red-blooded American male has been awaiting ever since the publication of the tease photos showing the wind lifting Marilyn Monroe's skirt above her shapely gams,' reported the *New York Daily Mirror*. The film confirms Marilyn's 'status as a fine comedienne. Her pouting delivery, puckered lips – the personification of this decade's glamour – make her one of Hollywood's top attractions,' the *Mirror* concluded. *The New Yorker* sniffed, 'When Miss Monroe turns up as a young lady too substantial for dreams, the picture is reduced to the level of a burlesque show, and Mr Ewell's efforts to be funny quietly are lost in the shuffle.'

If the repressed half of America was upset because Marilyn was too sexy and the fun-loving other half was happy that she was so dumb, both were astonished to hear what she was doing with her time while she absented herself from 20th Century-Fox. She was sitting in on classes at the Actors Studio. Since 1947, this shrine to the Stanislavski 'method' of acting has been where movie actors have pilgrimaged to become 'serious'. Marlon Brando, James Dean and Paul Newman have been among those who accepted the Studio's director Lee Strasberg as their mentor.

At first, Marilyn had shuffled in and out of classes at the Studio, saying nothing and sitting apart, a woebegone figure all in black. She would put her hands over her face, her shyness looking like aloofness. When she had to perform in front of other, better-trained actors, she didn't just glow or perspire, she sweated in fear. Another student at the time, Renee Taylor, recalled, 'Not once did I see in a movie – except perhaps *Bus Stop* – the range and talent she demonstrated in class no matter how nervous she was.' Marilyn steeled herself to perform scenes at the Studio from Eugene O'Neill's *Anna Christie*. With their applause, the other actors accepted her as one of them.

AN IMPERIOUS-LOOKING MARILYN WITH HER DRESSER. (KOBAL COLLECTION)

LEE STRASBERG. (KOBAL COLLECTION)

Strasberg flew in the face of all opinions when he took Marilyn as a private pupil in March 1955. He explained, 'I saw that what she looked like was not what she really was and what was going on inside was not what was going on outside, and that always means there may be something there to be worked with. It was almost as if she'd been waiting for a button to be pushed, and when it was pushed a door opened and you saw a treasure of gold and jewels.'

Strasberg remained the dominant artistic influence on Marilyn until she died. The question has often been asked whether he helped or harmed her. She was a better actress after 1955, most agree – but no one can say whether she would have become better if she'd never heard of Strasberg. Post-Strasberg, she was even harder to work with – but who can say whether her private demons would have intensified their attacks anyway?

After 1955, every Monroe movie was a Monroe vehicle. All of them bar *Let's Make Love* were made because Marilyn wanted to make them, but only one, *The Misfits*, was 'serious'. Despite all her talk about wanting to play dramatic roles, until *The Misfits* she never risked destroying her sexy image. But even though in the late 1950s Marilyn continued playing sexy characters, they were better-rounded sexy characters.

This distinction was possible because of the pack of copycat blonde bombshells, led by Jayne Mansfield and Mamie Van Doren, that was forming just downmarket of Marilyn at the apex of her fame as a sex symbol. These imitation Marilyns were necessarily parodies of Marilyn too. Their humour was broader, their physicality coarser. All angst eliminated, they were depthless reflections. But they were in demand and parts were being written for them.

While Marilyn was in New York in 1955, George Axelrod, who had written *The Seven Year Itch*, was producing a new play he'd written, *Will Success Spoil Rock Hunter?* It was a satire of the movie business, and its star was Marilyn Monroe – not really Marilyn, but 'a Marilyn Monroe type'. Mansfield played the part, which called for her to lie nude, lightly draped under a towel on a massage table, as the curtain went up. The play opened in October and ran for 452 performances. (Marilyn never attended.) Fox rushed to sign Mansfield for the movie version (retitled *Oh! For a Man!* in Britain). When Mansfield went West, Fox's publicity brains came up with a great campaign. Mansfield would break up with her sweetheart, a celebrated weightlifter named Mickey Hargitay, and supposedly go for a smart guy in glasses, somebody like quiz-show champ Charles Van Doren. Mansfield, who always claimed her IQ was 163, thought the parody of Marilyn's love life was a bit obvious and stuck with Hargitay.

Marilyn, meanwhile, was coming to terms with Fox, signing a new seven-year contract on 31 December 1955. She would make four pictures for Fox at $100,000 per picture, plus a profit percentage that could bring her company's income to $8 million, an enormous sum at the time. 'I'm happy to

OFF-SET ON *BUS STOP*, WITH JOSHUA
LOGAN. (KOBAL COLLECTION)

BUS STOP, WITH DON MURRAY. (KOBAL
COLLECTION)

(NATIONAL FILM ARCHIVE, LONDON)

be back,' she said. 'I have director approval. This is very important to me.' Marilyn's self-exile and holdout had gained all their objectives – she was even permitted to make one non-Fox film a year. In 1962, however, the Fox management that followed Zanuck had the last laugh when it fired Marilyn from her final film, the uncompleted *Something's Got to Give*.

In 1956, though, Marilyn was in her prime. She bewitched Joshua Logan, the director of her next picture, *Bus Stop*. Logan skilfully improvised around her eccentricities to extract what is arguably her best performance. George Axelrod's script re-worked William Inge's stage conception around Marilyn's personality, causing most to forget Kim Stanley, who created the character of Cherie on Broadway.

Logan, whose Broadway and Hollywood credentials were impeccable, was on Marilyn's short list of six approved directors for *Bus Stop*. But Logan hesitated. 'She can't act' was his original response to the idea of Marilyn playing Cherie. Urged by Lee Strasberg, whose daughter Susan he had directed in *Picnic*, Logan agreed to meet Marilyn for dinner at Milton Greene's Connecticut home. Marilyn took so long 'dressing' that she never appeared for dinner, but she eventually turned up and convinced Logan that 'She was Cherie, presto! in the flesh'. He found her much brighter than he expected, and was captivated by her wit and laughter. The deal completed, Logan became an employee of Marilyn Monroe Productions.

William Inge could have titled his story about a cheap singer and a bumptious cowboy *The Taming of a Bully*. The film follows the same storyline as many Marilyn movies: her innocence conquers all. In her first scene in *Bus Stop*, Marilyn announces, 'I'm a *chanteuse* – that's why I call myself Cherie.' When she sings 'That Old Black Magic', rumbustious cowboy Don Murray knows he's found what he needs, 'an angel, a real hootenany of an angel'. He slams into her hotel room to announce his intention to marry her, and he pursues her indefatigably and annoyingly in between rodeo triumphs. To escape him, she takes a bus out of town, but he climbs on too. Aboard the bus and at a diner where snow strands them overnight, he presses his suit. She says, 'I want a guy I can look up to and admire, but I don't want him to browbeat me . . . Whoever I marry will have real regard for me – aside from all that loving stuff.' Eventually Murray realizes that he's been a bully and wins Marilyn's heart by declaring that he doesn't care about her past. 'That's the sweetest, tenderest thing anyone ever said to me,' she says, and the match is made.

As with all Marilyn's star roles, Cherie was supposed to look and sound a lot like Marilyn. Anybody who knew about her relationship with DiMaggio and Miller – and that was everybody – made the connection between Marilyn's off-screen life and Cherie's line about wanting 'real regard'.

Joshua Logan and Arthur Miller differed somewhat in their recollections of Marilyn when she was making *Bus Stop* from February to May 1956.

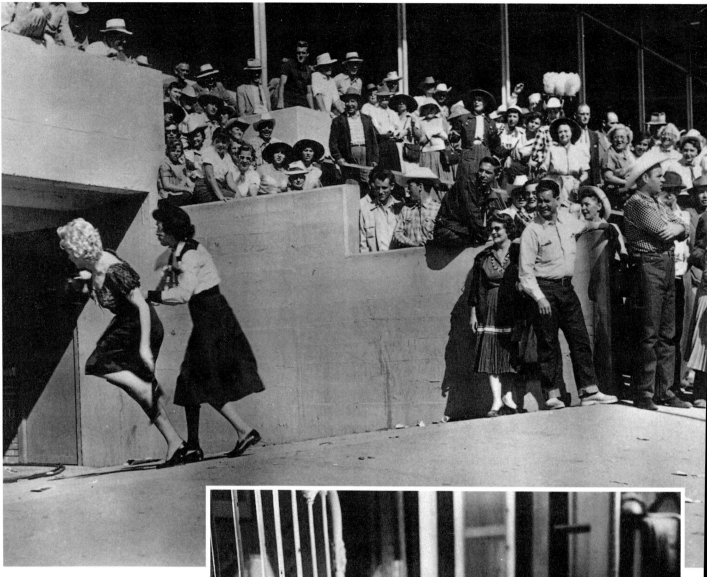

THE RODEO SCENE. (NATIONAL FILM ARCHIVE, LONDON)

(KOBAL COLLECTION)

Logan accentuated the positive atmosphere on the set, while Miller wrote about the despair Marilyn occasionally felt after a day's shooting. Her performance in the finished film might seem to justify Logan's rosier account. However, the fact that Marilyn interrupted filming for two weeks in April when she went into hospital suffering from 'virus infection, exhaustion, overwork and acute bronchitis' validates Miller's version.

At one point, Miller, who was in Reno establishing Nevada residency for his divorce, received a frantic late-evening phone call from Marilyn on the film's location in Phoenix. She complained that Logan didn't understand her. 'I can't work this way,' she wailed.

She mentioned a particular incident, a scene early in the film in which she runs across the rodeo arena where Murray has just roped a steer. Her shoe slips off, she darts back to retrieve it and then continues across. Logan recalled this as a bit of business – 'Marilyn's idea'. Marilyn, on the other hand, said that the shoe came off accidentally, and Logan was going to call 'Cut!' until he heard the crowd laughing. She said, 'I knew the minute it happened it would be good, and it was, but he doesn't know!'

Nevertheless, Logan did get the shot, and it was good. It was one of many occasions when Logan succeeded in manipulating Marilyn's spontaneity. Paradoxical though it sounds, this proved to be the approach that worked best with her. Shooting dialogue scenes, Logan would simply never turn the camera off. At the end of take one he would hand her whatever prop she was holding at the beginning of the scene or place her in her original position and call 'Action!' again. She would play the scene over and over until the film ran out. If she forgot a line, a prompter supplied it and she went on. Only once in the finished film did Logan fail to find a way to cut back and forth to conceal Marilyn's pauses.

Virtually all singing in films is pre-recorded in a sound studio. What we see on the screen is the performer 'lip-syncing' to a playback of the tune. Logan decided to shoot Marilyn singing 'That Old Black Magic' live, using two cameras. The result may lack smoothness, but it's probably Marilyn's best musical scene.

Whatever the tensions Marilyn reported in her calls to Miller, there were light moments on the *Bus Stop* set. On one occasion, the cameraman was lining up Murray for a close-up and said he couldn't see the top of Murray's head. Marilyn piped up, 'But everybody knows he's got one. It's been established.'

In the scene where Murray rushes into Marilyn's hotel room to announce that he's going to marry her, Marilyn insisted on being nude under the bedclothes. 'It's a nude scene. I've got to be nude in order to play the scene,' she explained. Marilyn came from her dressing-room to the set in a dressing-robe, which she removed after climbing into the bed. They began shooting the scene. On one take, Murray said she was 'pale and scaly' instead of 'pale and white', as the script read. Marilyn, who had spent the last year hearing a lot about psychology at the Actors' Studio, told Murray, 'You made a Freudian slip about a phallic symbol. You see, you were thinking unconsciously of a snake. That's why you said "scaly" and a snake is a phallic symbol. Do you know what a phallic symbol is, Don?' Murray answered, 'Do I know what it is? I've got one!'

TEN
'I hope you will all forgive me'

THE NEWLY MARRIED COUPLE IN ENGLAND. (LAURENCE OLIVIER AND VIVIEN LEIGH CAN JUST BE SEEN COMING THROUGH
THE DOORWAY BEHIND.) (POPPERFOTO)

*M*arilyn was a user – not just of drugs, for she also used people. She was the kind of person who was accustomed to getting what she needed from people and then, when they were out of sight, never afterwards giving them a moment's thought. There was always a replacement nearby, panting to be used in his turn. In her self-centredness, Marilyn was apparently unaware of this pattern. She always placed such high and usually unrealistic hopes on the new relationship that she forgot how and why the old one had ended.

As Joshua Logan swam out of view after *Bus Stop*, Laurence Olivier swam in. Logan never saw her again and Olivier soon wished he'd never seen her at all. In announcing her agreement to co-star with the man reputed to be 'the world's greatest actor', Marilyn was making a statement as well as expressing a propensity. It never hurt Miller's chances with her that many said he was 'America's greatest playwright'. In choosing to work with Olivier, even in a vehicle as frivolous as Terence Rattigan's boulevard comedy *The Prince and the Showgirl*, Marilyn was again acquiring some culture with a capital 'K'.

At her joint press conference with Olivier, Marilyn let it be known that the sort of part she aspired to play was Grushenka in Dostoyevsky's *The Brothers Karamazov*. 'She's a girl,' Marilyn joked. (Warner Brothers filmed the book the following year, with Maria Schell as Grushenka.)

Marilyn had admired high art from afar even before the Strasbergs communicated to her the aspirations of the legitimate stage (the term that used to denote non-burlesque in America). Marilyn had always carried weighty tomes around on film sets, but was rarely seen actually reading them. Most likely, these unread books were symbols of her yearnings. As Miller wrote in a more general context, 'She wanted to win recognition from men blinded to her humanity by her perfect beauty.' Of her actual reading accomplishments, Miller said he knew of just one book she read all the way through, Colette's 122-page *Cheri*.

At that New York press conference in June 1956, Dostoyevsky provided the words, and a broken shoulder strap on Marilyn's dress provided the pictures. It was an accident that Olivier remembered – he had Marilyn's character repeat the joke in the film, in the scene where she curtseys to the prince.

The Prince and the Showgirl was based on Rattigan's West-End hit play *The Sleeping Prince*, which, ironically, had starred Olivier's wife Vivien Leigh. Olivier said Leigh was 'really very sweet' about Marilyn taking her role. Marilyn had indeed taken it, for she and Milton Greene had initiated the joint production with Olivier. It was the first and only Marilyn Monroe Productions film made independent of Fox (it was released by Warner Brothers).

Marilyn plays an American chorine, Elsie Marina, who is in London at the time of the coronation of King George V in 1911. Olivier is Grand Duke

MARILYN WITH COLUMNIST SIDNEY SKOLSKY (ABOVE) AND HER DRESSER. (KOBAL COLLECTION)

Marilyn MONROE·

COURTESY OF

Dostoshi

AS ELSIE MARINA IN *THE PRINCE AND THE SHOWGIRL*. (NATIONAL FILM ARCHIVE, LONDON)

(NATIONAL FILM ARCHIVE, LONDON)

Charles, the Prince Regent of the (imaginary) kingdom of Carpathia, also there to see George V crowned. He watches her perform and goes backstage, where the stage manager is fretting, 'Will that girl ever make an entrance on time?' Invited to a little dinner à deux, Marilyn resists Olivier's clumsy advances and cheerfully wishes him 'Better luck next time, though not with me, of course.' Vodka and violins help change her mind, though she passes out before anything can happen.

The next morning Olivier is all statesman, dismissing Marilyn as 'a little American ninnycompoop'. Yet she gets the young king to confide in her and the dowager queen Sybil Thorndike to invite her to the Coronation. Olivier boils ('Don't you look cute when you're fierce,' she coos), but finds he must rely on Marilyn to solve his political difficulties. Now she is his 'pretty little dummkopf'. They declare their love but must part, he to Carpathia for the final eighteen months of his regency, she to work out her contract in her show.

Olivier embarked on the project in a flush of admiration. Summoned to New York, he gained admission to her apartment on Sutton Place (the swankiest little street in Manhattan). She was at home but did not appear. After an hour, Olivier eventually had to call to her through her door. When she at last showed herself, she gave him the full reduction-to-jelly treatment. The prospect of any difficulty directing this adorable, witty woman was the furthest thing from Olivier's mind when Marilyn arrived in London in mid-July, two weeks before the start of shooting.

She was at last Mrs Arthur Miller, having married the playwright on 29 June 1956. She had stood by Miller during his recent ordeal by congressional committee. After badgering him for two years, the House Un-American Activities Committee called him to Washington for a public hearing on his alleged Communist associations. While Miller was standing up to the congressmen's hectoring, Marilyn was staying quietly at Miller's lawyer's house. Some have written that Marilyn helped meet Miller's legal bills, but Miller didn't confirm this.

Once his HUAC ordeal was past, Miller could accompany Marilyn to London. He wouldn't just be holding her hand there. The West End's leading impresario, Binkie Beaumont, was going to back a production of Miller's *A View from the Bridge*, and Miller was to expand the play for this production.

The initial London press conferences promoting *The Prince and the Showgirl* established Marilyn as everyone's darling. As the woman of the hour, she was accorded the royal privilege of shopping at Marks and Spencer after hours to avoid a mob scene. But the newspapers soon followed the American press's pattern, vying to print stories about the 'real' Marilyn behind the posed smiles amid a sea of flashbulbs.

There was plenty to tell, for things did not go well at Pinewood Studios. One story Olivier didn't tell in his memoirs *Confessions of an Actor* was that to

ARTHUR MILLER, LAURENCE OLIVIER AND MARILYN PROMOTING *THE PRINCE AND THE SHOWGIRL*. (NATIONAL FILM ARCHIVE, LONDON)

help her relax while trying to remember lines, he suggested she count to three before saying the line. The trick didn't work and Olivier snapped, 'Can't you count, either?' The anecdote rings true, though; Miller observed that Olivier had 'an arch tongue, too quick with the cutting joke'.

The stage-trained Olivier, accustomed to leaving his neuroses at home, was perhaps the director least likely to get along with Marilyn since Otto Preminger, and he and his co-star were immediately at loggerheads. The 'all mucking in together' atmosphere on a British film set and the stand-up-and-do-it style of British acting were the opposite of Marilyn's experience. Olivier simply couldn't grasp the fact that Marilyn's foibles were non-volitional.

He had been warned. Joshua Logan had written to him about Marilyn, advising him against telling her how to read a line. He urged Olivier to stand by patiently and wait for her to find her own way to say the line. Logan particularly advised against letting Paula Strasberg on the set.

Paula Strasberg had become her husband's stand-in as Marilyn's on-the-set drama coach. Just as Marilyn once couldn't make a move without Natasha Lytess's nod, now she needed minute-by-minute guidance from Paula to supplement her daily long-distance phone talks with Lee. Paula Strasberg could earn $2000 a week for this service, though she would reiterate, 'I'm only Lee's representative.' The Strasbergs benefited further after Marilyn died – she willed Lee her rights to *The Prince and the Showgirl*.

Logan had allowed Strasberg to coach Marilyn in the star's dressing-room but had barred her from the set itself while Marilyn was working. For one reason or another, Olivier failed to make such a restriction stick. He found himself hardly able to communicate with his star except through this go-between.

Strasberg was roundly hated by everyone who had to work through her to get to Marilyn. Olivier scathingly concluded: 'Paula knew nothing; she was no actress, no director, no teacher, no adviser – except in Marilyn's eyes, for she had one talent: she could butter Marilyn up . . . "My dear, you are the greatest sex symbol in human memory . . . you are the greatest woman of your time, the greatest human being of your time, of any time, you name it. You can't think of anybody, I mean – no, not even Jesus – except you're more popular."'

Olivier thought Marilyn had learned more about acting from posing for stills photographers than from studying with Strasberg. He recalled her instantaneous responsiveness to his direction of the lengthy Coronation scene, which was performed without live sound, thereby permitting him to direct her verbally from behind the camera. He concluded that she wasn't so much an actress as a model.

Dame Sybil Thorndike expressed a different view: 'That little girl is the only one here who knows how to act before a camera.' Dame Sybil also recollected, 'She has an innocence which is so extraordinary, whatever she plays, however brazen a hussy, it always comes out as an innocent girl. I remember Sir Laurence saying one day during the filming, "Look at that face – she could be five years old."'

But when it came to getting through to this child-woman, Olivier was helpless. Before the film even began, he became exasperated by her inability to throw herself into rehearsals. Despite all his experience with American film-making, where nothing is rehearsed until just before it's shot and the leading man and leading lady are apt to play an intimate bed scene two minutes after meeting one another for the first time, Olivier had set aside two weeks for rehearsals. After failing to arouse Marilyn by rehearsing her directly, Olivier tried to rehearse Paula Strasberg, so she could rehearse Marilyn. Strasberg's limitations doomed that approach too.

Olivier had no way of knowing that he was up against not only Marilyn but also her drug habit. Unable to sleep when under stress, she resorted to pills that tended to stuporize her through most of the following day. The barbiturates contributed to her cloudy judgement, and she began seeing enemies everywhere.

When Strasberg went back to New York briefly and met difficulty trying to re-enter Britain, Marilyn believed Olivier and Milton Greene had pulled strings to spite her. Instead, Olivier had to pull strings to help her, and Strasberg was re-admitted. She thought Milton Greene was buying antiques in London and charging them against their joint company. Yet she had cheerfully authorized Paula Strasberg's travel to New York and back at her company's expense. Marilyn would break with Greene the following year after they had co-produced just two films. When the partnership was dissolved, Greene received a mere $100,000 payment.

The seeds of her estrangement from Miller were sown at this time, too, when she made it clear that she trusted him less than she did the Strasbergs. One justification for her change of heart towards Miller so soon after their marriage came when she found some notes Miller had written about her. She told the Strasbergs, 'It was something about how disappointed he was in me. How he thought I was some kind of angel but now he guessed he was wrong. That his first wife had let him down, but I had done something worse. Olivier was beginning to think I was a troublesome bitch and that he [Miller] no longer had a decent answer to that one.'

A scene recalling this episode appears in Miller's 1964 play *After the Fall*. The play, about a sex-kitten singer named Maggie married to an introspective writer named Quentin, contains many other echoes of Miller's relationship with Marilyn. The most obvious correspondence is Maggie's suicide. In addition, notes Christopher Plummer, who played Quentin in a 1974 television production, 'It [the writing] is fantastically accurate about Marilyn's speech patterns.' Miller claimed that he had all but finished the play at the time of Marilyn's death and insisted that he never concerned himself with any likenesses between Maggie and Marilyn. Still, audiences

and commentators saw Barbara Loden in a blonde wig on stage in 1964 and Faye Dunaway on TV ten years later and concluded that Miller either consciously or unconsciously wrote the play to justify himself.

After Olivier's bad beginning with Marilyn in rehearsals, things went further downhill. Marilyn was seeking the depths of her character's motivations, while he was concerned with placing her in the right spot in front of the camera. Though adept at flattery when required, Olivier was unable to provide the constant stream of uncritical reassurance that Marilyn seemed to demand. Reacting to Olivier's occasionally sharp comments and his tendency to be over-specific in his directing notes to her, Marilyn conceived the idea that Olivier was favouring his own performance. Olivier felt humiliated when he would offer Marilyn a piece of direction and she would turn to Strasberg for interpretation. He felt frustrated when she would demand extra takes after he pronounced himself satisfied with what he had already shot. He felt suicidal when she wouldn't respond to his most carefully prepared suggestions – and then would produce just the right note after consulting Strasberg. 'Honey, just think of Coca-Cola and Frankie Sinatra,' was the sort of cue from Strasberg that could somehow bring out the best in Marilyn.

At the end of the shoot, Olivier knew he hadn't done as well with Marilyn as he might have, and he blamed it on his fear of further arguments with her. At least Marilyn's tardiness had been manageable, and there had been only one prolonged absence – a week when Miller was in New York visiting his children from his first marriage. Marilyn had not worked that week because she was suffering from colitis, she said. Despite this, the film had been completed under budget, and Olivier decided to devote two days to re-shooting a few scenes, such as his and Marilyn's first meeting. He showed the spliced-together footage to Marilyn and Miller and pointed out the film's shortcomings. He got Marilyn to agree to arrive promptly and work quickly, which she did.

On its release, the film didn't justify Joshua Logan's prediction that the pairing of Olivier and Monroe was the greatest thing to happen in movies since black and white. But it did draw some favourable reviews, such as Alton Cook's in the *New York World Telegram* and *Sun*: 'She is captivatingly kittenish in her infectious mirth. Her love scenes are played as a girlish game.'

The on-screen and off-screen stories of *The Prince and the Showgirl* were thus very different. At the end of the dispute-filled shoot, before Marilyn returned to New York in November, she spoke to the cast and crew: 'I hope you will all forgive me, as it wasn't altogether my fault. I have been ill.'

ELEVEN

'I can't do it if it's not real'

(NATIONAL FILM ARCHIVE, LONDON)

*N*o director profited so much from hiring Marilyn as Billy Wilder did, and none was so cutting in his comments about her. Wilder thinks all human life is a subject for comedy, and he's willing to take back nine-tenths of what he says. When he finished shooting *Some Like It Hot* he sounded off: 'The question is whether Marilyn is a person at all or one of the greatest DuPont [chemical] products ever invented. She has breasts like granite, she defies gravity and she has a brain full of holes, like Swiss cheese. She hasn't the vaguest conception of the time of day . . . You can take forty-two takes of her in one scene and then you take her aside and say, to calm her down, "Don't worry, Marilyn", and she'll look at you with wide-open eyes and say, "Don't worry about what?"'

After directing Marilyn in *The Seven Year Itch*, Wilder had sounded terminally disenchanted with her, but when she expressed interest in *Some Like It Hot* in 1958 he found himself preparing to take more punishment from her. He and his co-writer I. A. L. Diamond had been building the project around the idea of Frank Sinatra playing Daphne, the role Jack Lemmon eventually took. At that stage, Sinatra was to be the star and Mitzi Gaynor would have played Sugar Kane. With Marilyn as the marquee name, however, Wilder could use a real comedian, Lemmon, to play Daphne.

Set during Prohibition in 1929, the film opens with a police raid on the speakeasy where Lemmon and Tony Curtis are playing bass and sax in the saloon's band. Put out of work, they're so poor they briefly consider joining an all-woman band before dismissing the idea as ridiculous. But after they witness George Raft perpetrate the St Valentine's Day Massacre, they're afraid of being rubbed out themselves. They decide to don feminine disguises and join Sweet Sue's Society Syncopators for a three-week engagement in Miami.

Marilyn is the band's singer and chief cut-up. On the train to Miami, she joins 'Daphne' for a drink in her berth. After their arrival, 'Josephine' (Curtis) finds a way to pursue Marilyn. He pretends to be a wealthy oil heir and lures her onto a yacht, where he induces her to kiss him by pretending to be impotent. Naturally, she 'cures' him. Daphne, meanwhile, has attracted the ardour of genuinely rich Joe E. Brown, whose yacht Curtis has borrowed. When the gangsters show up, Curtis and Lemmon elude them by taking a motorboat with their sweethearts to Brown's yacht. Marilyn forgives Curtis for not being rich and Brown forgives Lemmon for not being a woman, speaking the movie's famous tag-line, 'Nobody's perfect.'

Marilyn had spent the year and a half since completing *The Prince and the Showgirl* in a fortifying routine at Arthur Miller's side in New York. She continued working with Lee Strasberg. She saw her analyst virtually daily. At Miller's place on Long Island she would follow the fishermen along the beach, picking up gasping fish that they had dropped and throwing them back in the water. She was pregnant in the summer of 1957, but it was tubal and the pregnancy was terminated in August.

WITH ARTHUR MILLER, LEAVING HOSPITAL AFTER A MISCARRIAGE IN THE SIXTH WEEK OF PREGNANCY. (POPPERFOTO)

SWEET SUE'S SOCIETY SYNCOPATORS. (NATIONAL FILM ARCHIVE, LONDON)

AS SUGAR KANE, WITH JACK LEMMON. (NATIONAL FILM
ARCHIVE, LONDON)

WITH JACK LEMMON. (NATIONAL FILM ARCHIVE, LONDON)

The following July she was back in Hollywood, and the familiar disputes soon began, trying everyone's patience. She thought the movie should be in colour, but Wilder insisted on black and white because it was, after all, a gangster picture with George Raft, and Tony Curtis and Jack Lemmon might look too swishy in living colour. Marilyn decided that one of Lemmon's gowns would look better on her, causing designer Orry-Kelly to fume to Lemmon, 'She took your dress! The bitch has pinched your dress!' More ominously, one day during pre-production, Wilder needed the principals for camera tests. Marilyn was due at 1.00, arrived at 3.30 and was ready at 6.10. But Wilder had dismissed the crew at 6.00

When the film went into production, Marilyn's lateness became chronic. Rarely was she available for shooting before noon and often it would be well after lunch before she was ready. Wilder claimed she was driving him to drink, but he was too aware of her fragility ever to express his exasperation except through wisecracks. One time, she excused her delays by saying, 'I have to make contact with Sugar Kane.' Wilder tried to be gentle, 'Go ahead and make contact with Sugar Kane, but for God's sake, could you contact her a little faster?'

Marilyn's plaintive defence of her method was, 'I'm no trained actor. I can't pretend I'm doing something if I'm not. All I know is real. I can't do it if it's not real.' The difficulties on Marilyn's pictures weren't always related to her deficiencies in training or conduct. She had a nose for the right way to present her characters and the power to enforce her views. Marilyn didn't like the way Wilder shot her first scene in the film and forced him to re-shoot it, saying, 'I'm not going back into the fucking film until Wilder re-shoots my opening. When Marilyn Monroe comes into a room, nobody's going to be looking at Tony Curtis doing Joan Crawford. They're going to be looking at Marilyn Monroe.'

Wilder said of her, 'Here you have this poor girl and all of a sudden she becomes a famous star. So now these people tell her she has to be a great actress . . . They're trying to elevate Marilyn to a level where she can't exist. She will lose her audience. She is a calendar girl with warmth, with charm . . . Marilyn's whole success is she can't act . . . If she takes it seriously, it is the end of Monroe.'

Joking aside, he said of Marilyn's progress in the four years since he directed her in *The Seven Year Itch*: 'She has become a better actress, a deeper actress since Strasberg. But I still believe she was developing herself naturally and would have been greater even without him. I still say she was encouraged in her bad habits.'

One scene in *Some Like It Hot* typified Wilder's problems with Marilyn. He took some licence in his recollection: 'It takes her twenty seconds to say a line or make a move. For instance, she may have to make an entrance through a closed door. Two guys are playing a scene on this side of the door. The guys have twelve lines to speak and then she has to come in. So to get

SHOOTING A SCENE FROM *SOME LIKE IT HOT.*
(KOBAL COLLECTION)

POSTER ARTWORK SESSION FOR *SOME LIKE IT HOT*, WITH A STAND-IN FOR MARILYN. (KOBAL COLLECTION)

her to come in at the right time, which is after they are through speaking, I must press the light button for her cue to come in before they even say the first line.

'Maybe it's a psychological hurdle. I've noticed that if she gets past the first two or three lines she sometimes can go on and on, even if it's a long speech. She doesn't seem to get tired. She'll do take after take. She poops out the other actors. But Marilyn blooms as the day goes on, and she's at her best in the late afternoon, when the other actors are dropping like flies.'

In the scene in question, Marilyn comes into Curtis and Lemmon's room to locate some booze concealed in a rubber enema bag. She rummages through their bureau asking, 'Where's the bourbon? Oh, there's where it is!' The short scene went on and on. Marilyn simply could not say the line properly. She tried 'Where's the whisky?', 'Where's the bon-bon?', 'Where's the bottle?' Half as a joke, Wilder had the 'bourbon' line written on pieces of paper placed in the drawers of the bureau. Marilyn still blew the line. It had to be inserted later, and in the film it is heard while her back is to the camera.

Lemmon recalled betting with Curtis on how many takes this scene would require. He guessed fifteen but Curtis said, 'I smell a thirty-take coming on.' The number on the clapperboard kept rising and eventually reached fifty-nine.

'With this girl,' Wilder said, 'you may take a lot more takes than you think necessary, but when she's finally got a scene right, it's worth it.' The wonderful thing about Marilyn was that none of the problems she had making her films ever appeared on the screen. Stories abound about the horrific difficulties everyone experienced filming specific scenes with her – then you run the film and see the scenes and wonder what the fuss was about. Tony Curtis and Marilyn had some marvellously funny and romantic scenes in *Some Like It Hot*, yet Curtis recalled only agony while those scenes were being shot. Much screen time is devoted to Marilyn kissing Curtis ardently, yet those scenes only moved Curtis to make his comment about 'kissing Hitler'.

Lemmon was kinder in his recollections: 'I don't think Marilyn had a great talent. What she had was an ability to use completely the talents she did have . . . She built that into her unique personality and had incredible charisma . . . She had a good sense of comedy, but she had to bend the character to herself.

'I found that I couldn't really get to know what was inside her, despite a good working relationship. She would put up a glass window and never let anyone in. Anyone looking at her in retrospect could see that she was never really happy, never really fulfilled, never able to live with being Marilyn Monroe.'

Despite their 'good working relationship', Lemmon got no special favours from Marilyn. 'She had a tendency to act at instead of with you,' he recalled. 'She had a kind of built-in alarm system. It would "go off" in the

WITH TONY CURTIS. (KOBAL COLLECTION)

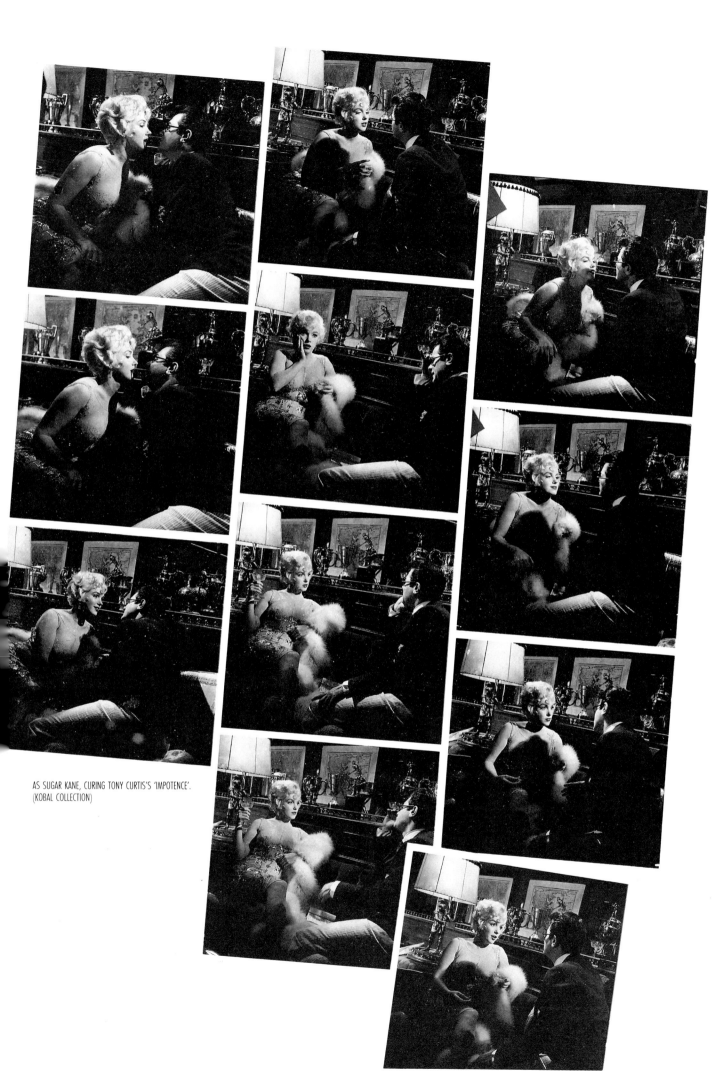

AS SUGAR KANE, CURING TONY CURTIS'S 'IMPOTENCE'.
(KOBAL COLLECTION)

middle of a scene if the scene was not right for her, and she would just stop everything. She wouldn't wait for the director to call "cut!" She just said "sorry", and she would stand there with her eyes closed, biting her lip, and kind of wringing her hands until she had it worked out. Now this sounds like selfishness, and I guess it is. But she didn't mean to be selfish – it was the only way she could work. Marilyn didn't give a damn about the director, the other actors or anything else. It would seem that she was doing exactly what she'd done the time before; but for her, something wasn't clicking quite right. I don't necessarily approve of the tactic; it was not easy working with her, but it was fascinating.'

Marilyn's frequent fits of hand-wringing were no 'Out, damned spot' tic but an exercise Lee Strasberg had given her to help relieve tension. The 'alarm system' that Lemmon noticed was, more likely, lapses in concentration caused by the lingering power of the previous night's tranquillizers – or possibly the new jolt she got from occasional nips from a thermos of vodka-laced orange juice she carried onto the set.

Location work at the Coronado Hotel near San Diego went more smoothly. These outdoor scenes had little dialogue, so Marilyn wasn't troubled by forgetting lines. Long shots predominated, so she had less need to worry about her hair and make-up.

Marilyn was two months' pregnant by the time the picture went into its last week in early November. Arthur Miller brought Wilder a doctor's note requesting that Marilyn be allowed to leave the set at 4.30 every day, due to her condition. Wilder replied, 'You get her here at nine ready to work and I'll let her go – no, not at 4.30 – I'll let her go at noon.' Immediately after filming ended on 6 November, Wilder threw a wrap party to which Marilyn wasn't invited. She couldn't have come anyway, for, twelve hours after the last shot, she began miscarrying, and she remained in hospital to be treated for her frequent ailment, 'nervous exhaustion'.

Some Like It Hot went over budget by more than half a million dollars, costing $2.8 million in the end. It grossed around $20 million. As Wilder said, 'That's the beauty of working with Monroe. She's not a parrot. Anyone can remember lines, but it takes a real artist to come on the set and not know her lines and give the performance she did.' Nobody's perfect.

TWELVE
'She is an enchanting child'

WITH YVES MONTAND. (NATIONAL FILM ARCHIVE, LONDON)

The contrast between Marilyn's aspirations and her actions is strongest in *Let's Make Love*, a piffling romance that was her last completed film at Fox. Whatever Billy Wilder said about her abilities and cooperativeness, after *Some Like It Hot* Marilyn should have been able to do better. But after splitting with Milton Greene she was unable to come up with self-packaged projects. Her addictions and emotional fragility kept her from working in two or three films a year, as many stars still did in the late 1950s. In the end, to fulfil her remaining obligations to Fox, she had to take whatever the studio wanted to force on her – which in January 1960 was *Let's Make Love*.

Marilyn had made up with Billy Wilder. The occasion was the arrival, on 19 September 1959, of Nikita Khrushchev at 20th Century-Fox. On a good-will US tour that ended with an all-smiles summit with Ike at Camp David, the Soviet leader had come to the centre of capitalist dream manufacturing to have lunch at the Fox commissary. Everyone was supposed to be there by noon. Wilder arrived fifteen minutes early and who should already be in her place but Marilyn Monroe, sitting next to Joshua Logan. Wilder's wisecrack: 'At last a man who can get Marilyn to come on time. Now I know who should direct all her pictures – Nikita Khrushchev.'

After the banquet, Marilyn embraced and kissed the gargoyle-faced Wilder. He said that bygones were bygones and they were 'good pals again'. He asked her to attend a sneak preview of his next film, *The Apartment*, starring Jack Lemmon and Shirley MacLaine. He said he wanted to consider her for a future project, *Irma La Douce* – a film he eventually made three years later with Lemmon and MacLaine.

In the second half of the Eisenhower era, America was beginning to grope towards the Continent for examples of how to break out of the stultifying conformity that encased its culture. Films like Vadim's *And God Created Woman*, Fellini's *La Dolce Vita*, Bergman's *The Seventh Seal* and Dassin's *Never On Sunday* astonished Americans accustomed to nothing racier than Rock Hudson and Doris Day. The studios' response was typical – they imported Continental stars to make otherwise totally American movies. Among them were Gina Lollobrigida, Sophia Loren, Anna Magnani – and Yves Montand.

Montand came to Hollywood at the urging of Arthur Miller, but their friendship came to an end during the filming of *Let's Make Love*, and Miller avoided mentioning Montand in his autobiography. A committed man of the Left, Montand starred with his wife Simone Signoret in the French production of Miller's play *The Crucible* for a year and even made a film of it, *The Witches of Salem*, in 1957.

Miller proposed Montand for *Let's Make Love* after half a dozen American leading men found something better to do than spend three months coping with Marilyn. The script had been written for Yul Brynner. Then Gregory Peck was supposed to do it. Turn-downs came from

WITH YVES MONTAND IN *LET'S MAKE LOVE*. (NATIONAL FILM ARCHIVE, LONDON)

ARTHUR MILLER, SIMONE SIGNORET, YVES MONTAND AND MARILYN DURIN[THE FILMING OF *LET'S MAKE LOVE*. (NATIONAL FILM ARCHIVE, LONDON)

WITH YVES MONTAND AT A PRESS PARTY. (POPPERFOTO)

Charlton Heston, Cary Grant, William Holden, Rock Hudson and James Stewart. To help make the deal with Montand happen, Miller even did some rewriting of the script.

The Millers and the Montands were such good friends at the start of filming in January 1960 that they took adjoining bungalows at the Beverly Hills Hotel. Soon Miller left to attend to business in Europe. Once when Miller called Marilyn from Europe, their conversation left her in tears. Montand and Signoret went next door to console her, and Signoret recalled, 'Suddenly I had in my arms a weeping girl who kept saying, "I'm bad, I'm bad, I'm bad. I won't do it again, I promise."' Of the two, Marilyn responded more warmly to Signoret at first. Marilyn's ability to manufacture hostility was beginning to sour her working relationship with Montand. One morning when she didn't show up at the studio, Montand went back to the hotel and wrote her a note that he slipped under her door: '. . . I'm not the enemy. I'm your pal. And capricious little girls have never amused me.'

When Signoret left to make a film in Europe and Miller remained abroad himself, Montand and Marilyn did not resist temptation. But when the film ended, the affair ended. Although Montand later confirmed the liaison, at the time he issued ambiguous statements like, 'I think she is an enchanting child, and I would like to see her to say goodbye, but I won't talk to her on the phone; somebody might be listening. I've never met anyone quite like Marilyn Monroe, but she is still a child. I'm sorry, but nothing will break up my marriage.'

Today the film seems merely an afterthought to the affair. Montand plays a millionaire playboy in New York who learns that an *avant-garde* theatre group is preparing a revue in which he will be parodied. His public relations man, Tony Randall, counsels that he play along with the gag instead of fighting it. Montand drops in on rehearsals and is immediately bewitched by Marilyn singing 'My Heart Belongs to Daddy'. She enters, sliding down a pole, and sings the Cole Porter standard while bumping and grinding vehemently. She closes by stripping off her sweater and tossing it into Montand's face. When the director takes Montand for an actor and auditions him for a bit part in the show, he's happy to seize this chance to be near Marilyn.

She gives him acting tips: 'Try acting with more assurance.' She gives him insights into himself: 'I feel sorry for you. You must have had a sad life.' He throws himself into the show. With his wealth, he hires Milton Berle to teach him to tell jokes, Bing Crosby to teach him to sing and Gene Kelly to teach him to dance. All the while, he pursues Marilyn. In the end, he's so desperate for her that he reveals his imposture – but she refuses to believe him. When Marilyn and the whole troupe descend on Montand's office to try and lift an injunction his conniving chief-of-staff has slapped on the show, she faints when she realizes that the pathetic would-be actor and the powerful multi-millionaire are one and the same. When she recovers she skitters into a lift but Montand calls it back and enters. Inside, he sings 'Let's Make Love' to her and she says 'Faker!' to him. She starts taking her clothes off. . . .

Afterwards, Marilyn said of the film, 'The worst part I had to play was *Let's Make Love*. I didn't even have a part . . . it was part of an old contract; I had nothing to say.' Marilyn was correct in saying she 'didn't even have a part'. Aside from her hot song and dance numbers (choreographed by Jack Cole), and the final scene in the lift, her character is a Miss Goody Two-Shoes. Her frigidity towards Montand is half-heartedly explained when Montand follows her home and finds out that her father is a clergyman. Otherwise, her character is an unappealing cypher. Paula Strasberg, in one of her pricelessly batty directions to Marilyn, advised her to kiss Montand 'as if it were cold water going over an iron fence', and the result on screen is uninvolving. Strasberg, by the way, at $2000 a week, cleared more than Marilyn on *Let's Make Love*.

Fox tried to publicize the film's alleged raciness by leaking an anecdote purporting to show how Marilyn got around the industry's censorship code. An official from 'the Brown office', as the censorship agency was known, came on the set to ogle a supposedly salacious number in which Marilyn and Montand sing the title song while kissing and writhing together, fully clothed, on a bed. It's a fantasy sequence in which Montand is imagining himself replacing the actor who is rehearsing this number with Marilyn for the show within the show. According to the story Fox put out, the censor objected to the number, saying that it showed two people obviously about to make love. Obviously. What clinched it for the censor was that the couple was horizontal. When Marilyn pointed out that it's equally possible to do it vertically, the censor had to agree and eventually passed the scene.

Director George Cukor reported that Marilyn's work habits seemed to have improved since *Some Like It Hot*. Her affair with Montand may have helped her overcome the pressures that usually made her difficult to work with. Nevertheless, Cukor did note some familiar problems: 'She couldn't sustain scenes. She'd do three lines and then forget the rest, she'd do another line and then forget everything again. You had to shoot it piecemeal.'

It took Cukor eleven days to shoot Marilyn's 'My Heart Belongs to Daddy' number, which takes six minutes on the screen. He attributed the delays to Marilyn's mixing up the 'daddy' in the title with Jim Dougherty. She had married Dougherty at sixteen and had called him 'daddy' (she liked to call Arthur Miller 'papa').

Like other directors before him, Cukor couldn't stay mad at Marilyn. 'I remember once she'd arrived late for work again, and I was annoyed, and then I watched her run across the stage in high heels (she always wore high heels), and it was so beautiful to watch, I just enjoyed watching her running and forgave her.'

Cukor remained in two minds about her. On the one hand, he said,

FILMING *LET'S MAKE LOVE*. (NATIONAL FILM ARCHIVE, LONDON)

LET'S MAKE LOVE. (NATIONAL FILM ARCHIVE, LONDON)

'I knew that she was reckless. I knew that she was wilful. She was very sweet, but I had no real communication with her at all. You couldn't get at her . . . As a director, I really had very little influence on her.' Nevertheless, as he recalled it, he found a way to handle her: 'I didn't try to treat her like I was her sugar daddy or to win her with my baby blue eyes. I just tried to create a climate in which she felt at ease and found it possible to work. She knew that I could help her deliver the goods if she trusted me.'

Analysing her appeal, Cukor said shrewdly, 'She had this absolutely unerring touch with comedy. In real life she didn't seem funny, but she had this touch. She acted as if she didn't quite understand why it was funny, which is what made it so funny . . . She invented this appealing baby voice. Also, you very seldom saw her with her mouth closed, because when it was closed she had a very determined chin, almost a different face. The face wasn't all that pretty, but it moved in a wonderful way. It was a wonderful movie face.'

THIRTEEN

'It was profoundly sad to see what was happening to her'

WITH CAMERAMAN RUSS METTY. (POPPERFOTO)

etween *Gone with the Wind* and *Cleopatra*, perhaps no film was so notorious before its release as *The Misfits*. The movie began as Arthur Miller's gift to Marilyn; it was shot amid rancour and distress and it ended with Clark Gable's death.

It was the first time since Marilyn had become a star that she worked extensively away from the protection of a studio lot, so she went through her customary agonies in full public view. *The Misfits* was perhaps the first film to inspire a contemporaneous 'the making of' book – John Goode's *The Story of the Misfits*. As often happens, by the time the film came out many moviegoers had heard so much about it that they felt they'd already seen it.

It was also one of the most expensive black-and-white films made up to that time, costing $4 million all told. Considering just the 'above the line' budget (acquisition costs plus principals' salaries), it was indeed the costliest black-and-white film to date. Gable alone earned $1.25 million up front ($750,000 plus penalties of $48,000 a week for going over schedule), and his estate got ten per cent of the gross.

The origin of the film was Miller's enforced stay in Reno in 1956 when he was getting the divorce that enabled him to marry Marilyn. He met some ageing cowboys who told him how they corralled wild horses and sold them for dogmeat. Miller wrote a story for *Esquire* about these lost souls and the 'misfits' they preyed on. Although Miller had had little directly to do with the movies up to then, he decided to turn *The Misfits* into a script after talking with John Huston when the director visited Marilyn in hospital in New York later in 1956. Miller wrote the part of Roslyn, the divorcee who falls in with the cowboys, with Marilyn in mind. On the strength of their commitments and Huston's interest, MCA agent George Chasin (who represented the Millers and Gable) made the deal with Seven Arts and United Artists, pending Gable's script approval.

Once Gable understood Miller's drift ('It's supposed to be a Western, but it's not, is it?' Gable asked at first), and Montgomery Clift sobered up enough to pass an insurance exam, producing was set to start in March. But a six-week Screen Actors Guild strike in March and April delayed the completion of Marilyn's *Let's Make Love* until 1 July. *The Misfits* couldn't start until 16 July, when the Nevada sun was most merciless.

As Miller explained to Gable, the film was an attempt to re-invent the Western. Westerns had fallen on hard times by the end of the 1950s, as TV-sated audiences had grown bored with their often simple-minded verities. But 'modern' Westerns like *The Misfits* and *Lonely Are the Brave* the following year never caught on either. It was left to Italian spaghetti Westerns to find the little life that remained in the spectacle of men on horseback doing what men have to do.

In Miller's new West, an Eastern woman named Roslyn Tabor (Marilyn) comes to Reno for a divorce from Kevin McCarthy. She meets untamed cowboy Gay Langland (Gable), who says of her, 'She's real prime.'

THE MISFITS. (NATIONAL FILM ARCHIVE, LONDON)

THE MISFITS: (LEFT TO RIGHT) MONTGOMERY CLIFT, ELI WALLACH, ARTHUR MILLER, JOHN HUSTON, CLARK GABLE AND MARILYN. (NATIONAL FILM ARCHIVE, LONDON)

THE CLOSING SCENE WITH CLARK GABLE.
(NATIONAL FILM ARCHIVE, LONDON)

FILMING *THE MISFITS*, WITH JOHN
HUSTON AND ARTHUR MILLER. (NATIONAL
FILM ARCHIVE, LONDON)

Marilyn and Gable set up housekeeping in an unfinished home outside of town provided by Gable's pal Eli Wallach. Marilyn fascinates both men. In a line that Miller said echoed something he once told Marilyn, Gable says, 'I think you're the saddest girl I ever met.' Wallach says, 'You have the gift for life; the rest of us are just looking for a place to hide.'

The two men plan a mustang roundup and set out for a nearby rodeo to pick up another hand. Montgomery Clift, low on dough, signs on. Marilyn wins a hatful of silver dollars in a saloon by skilfully paddling a rubber ball on the end of an elastic string. Clift hurts his head slightly in the rodeo and, emboldened by drink, tells Marilyn of his disinheritance. She consoles him, 'Maybe all there is, is the next thing that happens.'

They drive to the wild horse country, where Marilyn discovers what will happen to the mustangs. 'You know what you're doing isn't right,' she tells Gable. Gable's excuse: 'I hunt these horses to keep myself free.' Wallach flies a little plane that buzzes the horses out of the mountains, and Gable and Clift rope them from a truck. They hobble them and calculate their value at six cents a pound. In hysterics, Marilyn shouts at them, 'Killers! Murderers! Liars! You're only happy when you see something die!' Clift lets the horses go, but Gable single-handedly subdues the stallion before letting it go again. The two of them drive off together, Gable murmuring, 'Bless you, girl.'

By the time she began *The Misfits*, Marilyn was in the last stages of destroying her marriage to Miller. She was racked by second thoughts about the character of Roslyn, who she sometimes thought Miller intended less as a gift to her than a curse. For instance, she disliked the scene in which Roslyn expresses her outrage that the horses are to be killed. She said, 'I convinced them by throwing a fit, not by explaining anything. So I have a fit. A screaming crazy fit . . . And to think, Arthur did this to me . . . If this is what he thinks of me, well, then I'm not for him and he's not for me.'

Countering her doubts about Miller was a girlish delight in co-starring with Gable. As a fatherless child named Norma Jean, Marilyn had been consoled with a photo of Gable in her room and by the fantasy (implanted by her mother), that her real father was Gable. She said, 'My mother gave me a picture of him when I was a kid. She told me to pretend he was my father and I did. I became very close to that face. Gable became my fantasy. I dreamed of seeing him on the street but now I'll have him all to myself.'

For his part, Gable could only regard Marilyn as a wayward girl, for he and his fifth wife Kathleen (Kay) Williams were expecting his first child. Gable's stand-in Lew Smith said, 'Maybe Marilyn idolized Gable like a father, but she was in there pitching for more. She wanted him, if you know what I mean, and he was a big flirt and tease.' He called her by pet names like 'Chubby' or 'Fatso' or 'Beautiful'. While Marilyn chattered to her entourage about her desire to get Gable into bed with her, he would go no farther towards her than an occasional rump-fondle.

In one scene in the bedroom of the half-built house where the two are shacked up, Marilyn is nude under the covers when Gable comes in to wake her up. While shooting the scene, the sheet slipped on one take and Gable's hand brushed Marilyn's breast. He didn't react at all, but Marilyn talked about the incident afterwards as if it had been the high point of her erotic life to date: 'It was the most thrilling moment. When he kissed me, I wanted to go on and on and on. . . .'

Gable, the old pro, reacted less to Marilyn's come-on than to her chronic lateness. 'You'll probably see a lot of fire and smoke before we're through with this picture,' he warned. Because the deal for the film revolved around him, he was able to negotiate not only sky-high compensation but also a 9-to-5 working day. In a phone call to Joan Crawford, Gable complained, 'This fucking film. They're all nuts. Marilyn's never on time, if she shows up at all, so no one else gets here on time. We don't start shooting till afternoon, but goddam it, I leave at five, and that's it! The title pretty much sums this group up.'

Marilyn was rarely available before lunch and often absent or unable to work at all in the afternoon. So Gable had many idle hours to pass. Although witnesses reported that Gable never spoke harshly to Marilyn about her perpetual lateness, after his death his widow Kay put a different construction on matters. She said that the long periods of enforced idleness on the set and the consequent boredom led him to undertake many of his own stunts, which she said left him exhausted. 'It wasn't the physical exertion that did it. It was the horrible tension, that eternal waiting, waiting, waiting. He waited around forever, for everybody. He'd get so angry waiting that he'd just go ahead and do anything to keep active,' she said. This was the origin of the oft-heard statement that Marilyn somehow caused Gable's death.

Straining credulity somewhat, Marilyn countered, 'Why didn't he tell me? Why didn't he say anything? I'd have done anything for him. Anything! All he had to do was ask me to be on time. That's all. He always said, "It's all right, honey" – like he understood. If he asked me to be ready before dawn, that's what I would have done.'

During the long location shoot in Nevada, what remained of Marilyn's marriage collapsed. On and off the set her tirades against Miller were audible to all. Not long into the shoot she moved out of the rooms she shared with Miller and into Paula Strasberg's suite. Miller recalled the move as the physical manifestation of an emotional estrangement that had begun long before. In his eyes, Strasberg had 'won our long undeclared war'.

The short, fat Strasberg cut an absurd figure on the *Misfits* set. She had conceived the notion that black clothing was cooler in the sun-blasted Nevada summer, so she wore nothing but black, from black sandals to black straw hat. To some, she was like a character from a Charles Addams 'Munster' cartoon. The crew nicknamed her 'Black Bart'. One of Strasberg's perks was a personal air-conditioned limo, which she used not to travel to and from the set (she rode with Marilyn), but to while away the idle

WITH MONTGOMERY CLIFT. (KOBAL COLLECTION)

hours during shooting while everybody else except the principals sweltered.

Besides Strasberg, Marilyn travelled with a vast entourage: press agent, two hairdressers, a make-up man, 'body cosmetician', stand-in, masseur, secretary, wardrobe girl, seamstress and personal maid. Among this lot, Miller was *de trop*. But he remained on the set at least partly because Huston occasionally needed his services as screenwriter. Also, by then Miller had met the woman he was to marry later, Inge Morath, one of many journalists and photographers who came to Reno to cover the making of the film and experience what Miller called 'a force of pure destruction [that] was thrashing around among us, beyond anyone's control'.

Among the principals, Marilyn was closest to Monty Clift, an alcoholic homosexual whose troubles drew her sympathy. 'I look at him and see the brother I never had and feel brave and get protective,' Marilyn said. 'You should have seen them together,' said press agent John Springer. 'They were like two babes in the woods.'

The two Actors' Studio devotees had become soulmates two years before when Marilyn was shooting *Some Like It Hot* at Goldwyn Studios at the same time as Clift was shooting *Lonelyhearts* there. Clift had been sought to play the lead in *Bus Stop*, and an attempt had been made to cast them together in the roles Elizabeth Taylor and Paul Newman played in the 1958 film of *Cat on a Hot Tin Roof*. Later, Marilyn might have co-starred with Clift again in Huston's 1962 film *Freud*, but her analyst Dr Ralph Greenson cautioned against it, and Susannah York wound up playing the part of Freud's patient Cecily.

Clift's big scene with Marilyn in *The Misfits* is one of the movie's longest. It's the night after the rodeo, and he's wearing a comical turban-size bandage for his head wound. He rests his head on Marilyn's lap while she sits on a broken car seat outside a dance bar. Set at night, the scene was actually shot during the day behind black-out canvas. The extensive dialogue could have made the scene a nightmare to shoot, given the past unreliability of the two performers. Yet the master was shot in just six takes.

'Working with her was fantastic . . . like an escalator,' Clift said. 'You would meet her on one level and then she would rise higher and you would rise to that point, and then you would both go higher.'

Midway through the shoot, Marilyn's customary pill-induced semi-coma deepened, and she became virtually non-ambulatory. Miller described being let into Strasberg's suite one day and seeing a doctor giving Marilyn an injection in the back of her hand. The drug was Amytal, enough for a major operation, but Marilyn was so inured to it that she remained awake and repeatedly muttered to Miller, 'Get out. Get out.'

In his autobiography *An Open Book*, Huston recalled, 'Marilyn continued heavily into the drugs, and finally the young doctor on location refused to give her any more, even though he feared he might lose his job by not catering to her desires. She got drugs elsewhere, however, and

'WORKING WITH HER WAS FANTASTIC . . .' (NATIONAL FILM ARCHIVE, LONDON)

eventually she broke down completely and had to be sent to a hospital.' On 27 August Huston had her flown to Los Angeles to be detoxified. The usual 'acute exhaustion' story was fed to the press. Huston visited her in LA and found her chipper and contrite. The quick fix worked, and Marilyn returned to Nevada to resume shooting on 6 September. Huston made sure she was welcomed suitably at the airport but soon noted that she 'returned to her old ways as though she'd never had a break'.

One of Marilyn's old ways was forgetting her lines, but the familiar problem now had a new slant. *The Misfits* was a drama, not a comedy like *Some Like It Hot*, the humour of which was dependent on the timing embedded in the precise words of the script. Marilyn had to say the dialogue correctly in Wilder's film, but on Huston's she could claim that getting the feelings right was more important than getting the words right. Huston raised her hackles by insisting on word-perfect line readings. He also demonstrated a lordly disdain for Paula Strasberg, even after Lee Strasberg flew in from New York to try and enhance her position on the set.

Huston's strength as a director was realism. His stories generally fell into genres that appeal to men, and in his movies actresses rarely had the best roles. His style of directing seemed best suited to men who needed no coddling, like Bogart, Connery and Gable. He treated Marilyn as a professional even when she wasn't, making elaborate displays of patience no matter how difficult she was, even when he himself was unravelling after another night spent dicing at Reno's craps tables. Huston sometimes got what he needed despite her. In at least one long shot of Marilyn, Huston 'stole' the shot, running the camera without telling Marilyn he was shooting her.

'When she was herself,' Huston wrote, 'she could be marvellously effective. She wasn't acting – I mean, she was not pretending to an emotion. It was the real thing. She would go deep down within herself and find it and bring it up into consciousness. But maybe that's what all truly good acting consists of. It was profoundly sad to see what was happening to her.' Huston concluded, 'She had no technique. It was all the truth, it was only Marilyn. But it was Marilyn, plus. She found things, found things about womankind in herself.'

In mid-October the unit left Nevada to shoot interiors and pick-ups at Paramount. The last shot, on 4 November, was a re-take of Gable's and Marilyn's last scene, in which Gable lets Marilyn out of his truck so she can bring along the dog he might have left behind. It was a process shot, in which a loop of landscape played on a screen behind the actors.

Midway through the film, Gable had some dialogue that remains haunting: 'Honey, we all got to go sometime, reason or no reason. Dying's as natural as living. Man who's afraid to die is too afraid to live.' On 5 November, the day after he finished that last shot with Marilyn, Gable had a heart attack. He died eleven days later. No one knew the scene would be Marilyn's last, too.

FOURTEEN

'In the end I found that I could no longer reach her'

TESTS FOR *SOMETHING'S GOT TO GIVE*. (KOBAL COLLECTION)

*M*arilyn divorced Miller two months after she finished *The Misfits* and began the desperate slide into incapacity that ended with her death in August 1962. She spent time in a psychiatric ward in 1961. Afterwards, the only studio that would bet on her employability was Fox. One possible film for Marilyn was George Axelrod's *Goodbye, Charlie*, as the reincarnation of a dead gangster (the part eventually played by Debbie Reynolds in the 1964 film). In the end, Fox decided to reach into its old bag of tricks for another remake – *Something's Got to Give*, with Marilyn and Dean Martin in the roles Irene Dunne and Cary Grant had played in the 1940 *My Favourite Wife*. George Cukor, who had coped adequately with Marilyn on *Let's Make Love* two and a half years before, was assigned to direct, with a start-date in mid-May 1962.

No studio was more aware of Marilyn's foibles than Fox, so it was never contemplated that the film would shoot on any location. The principal set was to be a Beverly Hills mansion. There are many mansions in Beverly Hills, and some householders are happy to collect thousands of dollars a day renting to film-makers. But after *The Misfits*, Fox knew Marilyn would have to be kept behind studio walls, where the noonday sun always shines. Accordingly, Fox built a mansion on its lot. The model for the mansion in the movie was George Cukor's own home, complete with swimming pool.

Cukor explained, 'If she were very late coming to the location, we would lose the afternoon sunlight before we finished a scene. So it was simpler in the long run to build the exterior of the hero's house in the studio. My house was used as a model for the house, so that the scenic designer could measure its dimensions and then construct the set to scale on the sound stage in a hurry.'

The story Cukor never finished filming had Marilyn, a long-lost explorer, returning to her husband to find him recently re-married. He dithers over how to tell his new wife about his former wife and then dithers some more over which wife he should keep. Marilyn brought two things to the plot that Irene Dunne couldn't – the ability to sing and the willingness to do a pool scene nude. Dunne got pushed into a pool fully clothed, but the one still from the re-make that Fox distributed showed a mostly immersed and presumably nude Marilyn peeking over a pool's edge.

Of the film's short production, Cukor recalled, 'Marilyn was more or less on time when we made *Let's Make Love*. But when we were making *Something's Got to Give*, her preoccupation with her emotional difficulties made it an agony for her to come to the studio at all; and even when she did, she might get sick or fall asleep in her dressing-room and fail to report to the set anyhow. I think she knew that she wasn't doing a good job when she did play a scene, and she therefore became more and more terrified of facing the cameras, with the result that she would look for any excuse not to.

'Her behaviour often seemed bullying, as if she was simply being wilfully unaccommodating in keeping everyone waiting for her. But she

TESTS FOR *SOMETHING'S GOT TO GIVE*. (KOBAL COLLECTION)

SOMETHING'S GOT TO GIVE. (POPPERFOTO)

wasn't deliberately heedless, though practically speaking I suppose it came to that. It's sad, but she infuriated just about everyone. And in the end I found that I could no longer reach her.'

No one else could, either. Since Marilyn and Miller parted, the biggest of her 'emotional difficulties' was her relationship with Robert F. Kennedy. This bizarre connection was Marilyn's third reach for the brass ring in a field outside Hollywood. In Gloria Steinem's phrase, she had attempted to 'absorb the images' of baseball's Joe DiMaggio and drama's Arthur Miller. Now there was the attorney-general of the United States, the brother of the president. In fact, Marilyn had been passed on to Bobby by Jack, who had used her briefly as he had so many other girls supplied to him by various shady characters.

These were deep waters indeed, but Marilyn plunged in unheeding. She had agreed to a ridiculous publicity stunt on 29 May, just before starting *Something's Got to Give* – riding into Madison Square Garden in New York on an elephant and leading the assembled mob in singing 'Happy Birthday' to the president. One of the president's men, Arthur Schlesinger Jr, wrote that Bobby would meet her at Peter Lawford's house, and that she would call him in Washington. 'She was very often distraught,' Schlesinger wrote. 'One feels that Robert Kennedy came to inhabit the fantasies of her last summer.' She imagined that Bobby would somehow throw over his wife and career for her – after all, Miller had basically done that. But by the time she was making *Something's Got to Give*, Bobby had disengaged himself from her. He was no longer even taking her calls.

Her despair at the end of this affair was the background to the débâcle of *Something's Got to Give*. At the time, the studio was in turmoil as the extent of its $30 million losses on *Cleopatra* became known. Three weeks into shooting *Something's Got to Give*, production was suspended and Marilyn was fired. In those three weeks, she had been able to work often enough and well enough to contribute to just one week's worth of usable footage. Peter Levathes, head of production, took the decision to fire Marilyn. After dallying briefly with the idea of hiring Jayne Mansfield or Lee Remick or bringing in Jean Negulesco to replace the exasperated Cukor, Levathes cancelled the film altogether, swallowing a $2 million investment. The only return Fox got was the footage it used in the documentary/compilation film *Marilyn* that the studio released in 1963 (none of Marilyn's non-Fox films is represented).

'Once I learned all the facts,' Cukor commented, 'I could understand in retrospect that Marilyn had done all she could to cooperate on the film. Poor Marilyn was very irritating to work with, but she was a complicated, rather touching creature, and I liked her. When she took her life only a few weeks after the picture was shut down, I should have thought that her suicide explained only too clearly that she was too preoccupied with her own private mental anguish to make our movie.'

THE KENNEDY BROTHERS IN 1958. (POPPERFOTO)

Cukor could understand because the studio paid him off, but the crew of the film lacked that aid to understanding. Many who had worked on the cancelled film and were now between jobs signed an advertisement in the trade paper *Variety* ironically thanking Marilyn. Fox shrugged and went on the following year to re-launch the re-make with Doris Day and James Garner, this time calling it *Move Over Darling*.

Marilyn made a few half-hearted efforts through friends in the press to re-establish her viability. She spoke of *Something's Got to Give* as if it might be re-started at any time and as if she had no idea why it had been shut down: 'I did everything they asked me to. When the director said the swimming pool scene in the picture would look more realistic if I did the scene in the nude, I agreed – because I was told it would make the picture more of a success artistically and commercially. I worked very hard . . . I wanted it to be a great picture, believe me. Everything they've been saying in the press is untrue. I hope we can continue . . . It can be a great picture – I know it can and so does everyone else. But all I can do is wait until they let me know.'

She moved to a rented home in Brentwood. She was surrounded by people employed to look after her welfare, including a live-in psychiatric nurse. On 4 August she argued with her press agent after the agent had taken away her sleeping pills. That afternoon she spent two hours with her psychiatrist Dr Ralph Greenson, who recalled her as 'confused and distraught'. She was dressed only in her robe.

Later, Peter Lawford called to invite her to dinner – she never went. At 9.30 the nurse came to Marilyn's bedroom door, saw the light on and the telephone cord under the door and assumed everything was all right. Long after midnight, the nurse became alarmed and called Dr Greenson. Greenson broke down Marilyn's door. She was naked, holding the phone. And she was dead.

FIFTEEN

'She always thought they were cheering for someone else'

MARILYN IN *RIVER OF NO RETURN*. (NATIONAL FILM ARCHIVE, LONDON)

*M*arilyn had taken an overdose of Nembutal and chloral hydrate pills. Her death was ruled a suicide, but because she didn't leave a note many have refused to believe this verdict. Conspiracy theorists have alleged but never proved that the government or the Mafia killed her. Others have said that she didn't mean to kill herself. John Huston, for example, wrote, 'She killed herself by accident . . . I'm sure she never meant to take her life.' The truth will probably never be known.

A glamorous, mysterious death is a sure route to immortality in a place like Hollywood, where imaginings sometimes seem more substantial than realities, and stars like Marilyn attract phrases like Norman Mailer's 'the sweet angel of sex'. Even among those who should know better, the movies' prime personalities are more revered for what they symbolize than for who they are. Their actual lives are of interest only insofar as they support the image. Real events in stars' lives are quickly reinterpreted to serve the myth.

To many at the time, Marilyn's death seemed appropriate. Her 'suicide' brought down the curtain of the morality play called *Marilyn* that most people were watching in their heads. This one-act play climaxed at just the right moment. It could have been subtitled, quoting F. Scott Fitzgerald, 'There are no second acts in American lives.'

The morality play had a message: Marilyn deserved to die because she was bad. She had to kill herself because she knew she was bad and was sorry. She couldn't help being bad. She was born bad and learned to enjoy being bad. If fact, she made being bad her business. But it was a deal with the devil. She could only be truly bad as long as she was young and beautiful. An early death was part of the bargain.

Recalling Marilyn, George Cukor used the word 'mad' instead of 'bad'. He said, 'There may be an exact psychological term for what was wrong with her . . . I think she was quite mad. The mother was mad, and poor Marilyn was mad . . . She was very observant and tough-minded and appealing, but she had this bad judgement about things. . . .' As Robert Mitchum said, 'She always thought they were cheering for someone else.'

Mad or bad, Marilyn couldn't help herself. At that time, such a life could not end well. Consider the difference between Marilyn and her doppelganger, Jayne Mansfield. Mansfield's career was parodying Marilyn – on stage, in the movies and in her poses for the paparazzi. Mansfield emphasized the fact that her blondeness came from a bottle. Her bosom was almost grotesquely large. Her sayings were almost camply provocative. She was pneumatic where Marilyn was real flesh. When Mansfield died in a car crash in 1967, her play was already over in the public consciousness. After her death, we couldn't forget her quickly enough.

Appropriate as Marilyn's death seemed, we buried her in sorrow, as if she'd been a child we'd let run too free. And later, after Andy Warhol and other pop archivists kept reminding us of how compelling certain images of her remained, we began to feel her loss even more personally. We began to

THE SEVEN YEAR ITCH. (NATIONAL FILM ARCHIVE, LONDON)

understand that in asserting the joyousness of naked sensuality, standing over that subway grating on Lexington Avenue in her white halter dress, laughing as the on-rush of warm air tickled her legs, Marilyn had been taking the heat for all of us.

Very soon after Marilyn's death, the social changes that we label the sexual revolution and the women's movement gave us a new perspective on her. In the 1950s, few would have quarrelled with Darryl F. Zanuck's wounding remark that she was 'just another easy lay', for Marilyn deliberately gave that impression. Marilyn seemed to accept society's verdict of her, even though calling a woman an 'easy lay' was like calling a man a thief and a coward. In the late 1960s, Hollywood and the rest of society began adopting a more open attitude towards sex. Everybody became more like Marilyn had seemed to be. Overnight, virtually all of Marilyn's scenes on film, having been based on the assumption that sex is too much fun actually to have any, became period pieces. Most of what had been said about her suddenly seemed from the Stone Age.

In the early 1970s, feminists began citing her life to show how sexism objectifies and infantilizes women, especially beautiful women. From one kind of remote symbol, Marilyn became another – 'Saint Marilyn', in Billy Wilder's withering phrase. Even so, it became apparent how few of Marilyn's difficulties were consciously willed and how many were socially determined. The more we found out about her addictions and mental illnesses, the more human she seemed. As we saw more and more public figures admit to the kind of problems Marilyn had to hide, and get the kind of treatment and understanding that weren't available to her, we revered her less as a goddess than we sympathized with her as another erring mortal. We know gods must die, and we're glad they die for us. People don't have to die the way Marilyn did, and her death now seems a tragic waste. It was not appropriate. The play ought to have run for ever.

'To have survived,' Arthur Miller wrote, 'she would have had to be either more cynical or even further from reality than she was. Instead, she was a poet on a street corner trying to recite to a crowd pulling at her clothes.'

We're left with the enduring Myth of Monroe. Angela Carter, a writer concerned almost exclusively with interpreting myths, concluded, 'The essence of the physicality of the most famous blonde in the world is a wholesome eroticism blurred a little round the edges by the fact that she herself is not quite sure what eroticism is. This gives her her tentative luminosity and makes her, somehow, always more like her own image in the mirror than she is like herself.'

Marilyn's career – her actual movies – is little remembered today. Most of the time she played characters that were too child-like or one-note glamorous to allow the tragic strain of her character to appear. What we respond to in her now is rarely glimpsed on the screen, except in *The Misfits*, which remains a riveting if too-talky film. Of the films she starred in, only

Some Like It Hot shows any signs of achieving immortality on its own merits. *The Asphalt Jungle* and *All About Eve* are classics, gaining only the slightest cachet from Marilyn's appearances in bit parts.

It's ironic, but Marilyn has become more revered for her stills than for her actual movies – just as she is more pitied for her tragic loves than for the loss of a career that might have extended into middle age. At the time of her death, it seemed better that she never had to try and prove she could play characters who didn't have to be glamorous. Yet others who followed her made that transition, such as Elizabeth Taylor and Sophia Loren. If things had worked out differently, would Marilyn at sixty-three be starring in *Dynasty* today?

Filmography

(listed by date of US release)

1948	*Scudda Hoo! Scudda Hay!*
	Dangerous Years
1949	*The Big Wheel*
	Ladies of the Chorus
1950	*Love Happy*
	A Ticket to Tomahawk
	Right Cross
	The Fireball
	All About Eve
	The Asphalt Jungle
1951	*Hometown Story*
	As Young As You Feel
	Love Nest
	Let's Make It Legal
1952	*Clash by Night*
	We're Not Married
	Don't Bother to Knock
	Monkey Business
	O. Henry's Full House

1953	*Niagara*
	Gentlemen Prefer Blondes
	How to Marry a Millionaire
1954	*River of No Return*
	There's No Business Like
	Show Business
1955	*The Seven Year Itch*
1956	*Bus Stop*
1957	*The Prince and the*
	Showgirl
1959	*Some Like It Hot*
1960	*Let's Make Love*
1961	*The Misfits*
1962	*Something's Got to Give*
	(uncompleted)

Selective Iconography

The following is a list of a few of the instances in which Marilyn Monroe's image has been used in books, movies, plays, songs and advertisements. Some are serious efforts at biography, others are affectionate homages, a few are business transactions. As Quentin says to Maggie in Arthur Miller's *After the Fall*, 'It's not the money they take; it's the dignity they destroy.'

1955   *Will Success Spoil Rock Hunter?* Broadway comedy about Hollywood by George Axelrod. Jayne Mansfield played a part based on Marilyn.

1958   *How to Marry a Millionaire* TV series based on the 1953 movie. Barbara Eden played the Marilyn part.

1963   *Marilyn* A compilation film of Marilyn's work for 20th Century-Fox.

1964   *After the Fall* produced in New York.

1966   *The Symbol* A novel by Alvah Bessie fictionalizing Marilyn's life.

1973   *Candle in the Wind* Song by Elton John, co-written by Bernie Taupin.

1974   *The Sex Symbol* Film version of Alvah Bessie's novel made for ABC by Columbia. Connie Stevens played the Marilyn figure. Shelley Winters and Don Murray also starred. Ninety-eight-minute version released in cinemas abroad. Seventy-four-minute version shown on US TV.

1975   *Legend* Play about Marilyn's life by David Butler produced in England. Sandra Dickinson played Marilyn.

1976   *Goodbye Norma Jean* Film of Marilyn's early life directed by Larry Buchanan. Title comes from the opening line of Elton John song. Misty Rowe played Marilyn.

1980   *This Year's Blonde* (also distributed as *The Secret Love of Marilyn Monroe*) Warner Brothers television film for NBC based on Garson Kanin's *Moviola*, a fictionalized account of actual Hollywood incidents. The film centred on Marilyn's relationship with agent Johnny Hyde, played by Lloyd Bridges. Constance Forslund played Marilyn.

1980   *Marilyn: The Untold Story* Film for ABC television produced and co-directed by Lawrence Schiller from Norman Mailer's book. Catherine Hicks played Marilyn. Sheree North played Marilyn's Aunt Gladys.

1983   *Remember Marilyn* Shops opened at Bloomingdale's department stores in New York and suburbs, offering a line of blouses, sweaters and tight pants.

1983   *Marilyn!* Musical about Marilyn's life produced in England. Music by Mort Garson. Book and lyrics by Jacques Wilson. Stephanie Lawrence played Marilyn.

1985   *Insignificance* Film directed by Nicolas Roeg fictionalizing the night Marilyn shot the subway grating scene in *The Seven Year Itch*. Theresa Russell played the Marilyn figure.

1985   *Marilyn, Say Goodbye to the President* Seventy-one-minute BBC documentary written and directed by Christopher Olgiati speculating on a possible political cover-up of the circumstances of Marilyn's death.

1987   *Hoover vs. the Kennedys: The Second Civil War* Film for US cable television. Heather Thomas played Marilyn.

1988   *Marilyn Monroe: Beyond the Legend* One-hour documentary narrated by Richard Widmark, containing film clips and interviews with Robert Mitchum, Joshua Logan, Susan Strasberg and others.

1988   *Remembering Marilyn* One-hour documentary for ABC television containing film clips and interviews. Lee Remick hosted.

1988   Holsten Pils advertisement in which actor Griff Rhys Jones plugs Holsten while superimposed on a scene of Marilyn in *Some Like It Hot*.

1988   *License the Legend* Advertisement headline in the *Wall Street Journal*. The ad by the Roger Richman Agency offers exclusive merchandizing, advertising and promotion licences and says more than sixty companies already have taken out such licences.

Selective Bibliography

Arnold, Eve. *Marilyn Monroe – An Appreciation.* Knopf. 1987.
Bacall, Lauren. *Lauren Bacall: By Myself.* Knopf. 1978.
Baltake, Joe. *Jack Lemmon.* Citadel Press. 1977.
Conway, Michael and Ricci, Mark. *The Complete Films of Marilyn Monroe.* Citadel Press. 1968.
Cotten, Joseph. *Vanity Will Get You Somewhere.* Mercury House. 1987.
Eells, George. *Robert Mitchum.* Franklin Watts. 1984.
Essoe, Gabe. *The Films of Clark Gable.* Citadel Press. 1970.
Freedland, Michael. *Jack Lemmon.* St Martin's Press. 1985.
Guiles, Fred Lawrence. *Norma Jean: The Life of Marilyn Monroe.* McGraw. 1968.
Guiles, Fred Lawrence. *Legend: The Life and Death of Marilyn Monroe.* Stein & Day. 1984.
Harris, Warren G. *Cary Grant.* Doubleday. 1987.
Hunter, Allan. *Walter Matthau.* St. Martin's Press. 1984.
Huston, John. *An Open Book.* Knopf. 1980.
Kahn, Roger. *Joe and Marilyn: A Memory of Love.* Morrow. 1986.
LaGuardia, Robert. *Monty.* Arbor House, 1977.
Lambert, Gavin. *On Cukor.* Putnam. 1972.
Leaming, Barbara. *Orson Welles.* Viking. 1985.
Logan, Joshua. *Movie Stars, Real People, and Me.* Delacorte. 1978.
Luijters, Guus. *Marilyn Monroe: A Never-Ending Dream.* St Martin's Press. 1987.
Mailer, Norman. *Marilyn.* Grosset. 1973.
Marill, Alvin H. *Robert Mitchum on the Screen.* Barnes. 1978.
Martin, Pete. *Will Acting Spoil Marilyn Monroe?* Doubleday. 1956.
Marx, Arthur. *The Nine Lives of Mickey Rooney.* Stein & Day. 1986.
Merman, Ethel, with Martin, Pete. *Who Could Ask for Anything More?* Doubleday. 1955.
Miller, Arthur. *Timebends.* Grove Press. 1987.
Monroe, Marilyn. *My Story.* Stein & Day. 1974.
Mosley, Leonard. *Zanuck: The Rise and Fall of Hollywood's Last Tycoon.* Little, Brown. 1984.
Noguchi, Thomas, with DiMona, Joseph. *Coroner.* Simon & Schuster. 1983.
Olivier, Laurence. *Confessions of an Actor.* Weidenfeld & Nicolson. 1982.
Paar, Jack, with John Reddy. *I Kid You Not.* Little, Brown. 1959.
Pepitone, Lena, and Stadiem, William. *Marilyn Monroe Confidential.* Simon & Schuster. 1979.
Phillips, Gene D. *George Cukor.* Twayne. 1982.
Preminger, Otto. *Preminger.* Doubleday. 1977.
Russell, Jane. *My Path and My Detours.* Franklin Watts. 1985.
Sanders, George. *Memoirs of a Professional Cad.* Putnam. 1960.

Saxton, Martha. *Jayne Mansfield and the American Fifties.* Houghton Mifflin. 1975.
Smith, Ella. *Starring Miss Barbara Stanwyck.* Crown. 1985.
Steinem, Gloria. *Marilyn, Norma Jean.* Henry Holt. 1986.
Summers, Anthony. *Goddess.* Macmillan. 1985.
Thomas, Bob. *I Got Rhythm: The Ethel Merman Story.* Putnam. 1985.
Thornabene, Lyn. *Long Live the King.* Putnam. 1976.
Trescott, Pamela. *Cary Grant.* Acropolis. 1987.
Warren, Douglas. *Betty Grable.* St Martin's Press. 1981.
Wayne, Jane Ellen. *Gable's Women.* Prentice-Hall. 1987.
Wayne, Jane Ellen. *Stanwyck.* Arbor House. 1985.
Widener, Don. *Lemmon.* Macmillan. 1975.
Winters, Shelley. *Shelley: Also Known as Shirley.* William Morrow. 1980.
Wood, Tom. *The Bright Side of Billy Wilder, Primarily.* Doubleday. 1970.
Zolotow, Maurice. *Marilyn Monroe.* Harcourt Brace Jovanovich. 1960.
Zolotow, Maurice. *Billy Wilder in Hollywood.* Putnam. 1977.

Index

Page numbers in *italic* refer to the illustrations